# GUIDESTONES:

## Ancient Landmarks of Authenticity for the 21st Century Church

# O. S. HAWKINS

**GuideStone**
FINANCIAL RESOURCES
of the Southern Baptist Convention

# OTHER BOOKS BY
# O. S. HAWKINS

# DEDICATION

## To David Shivers

*Husband of our daughter, Holly; father of our grandchildren, Jackson and Julia; faithful minister of the Gospel of the Lord Jesus Christ. His genuine care and concern for others and his passion for winning the lost to Christ inspire me every day to become more like Christ myself.*

# TABLE OF CONTENTS

*Roman Guide Stone*

# FOREWORD

The first century church of the New Testament world lived and ministered under the iron fist of the occupation of the Roman Empire. In their age-old conquest for world dominion the Romans had built an elaborate system of super highways throughout the empire. These roads were architectural miracles in their excavation and engineering. They stretched for fifty thousand miles!

At every mile along these roads was a stone marker that pointed direction, determined distance to the next town and warned of dangers which might lie ahead. Each of these markers not only gave the mileage to the next town or village but also to Rome. Thus, the familiar saying, "all roads lead to Rome." And, in the first century world they did exactly that. The *Oxford English Dictionary* defines a "guide stone" as a marker for travelers and relates that its most common usage was in Roman times as a directional, distance and danger marker placed along the endless miles of the Roman roads. These stones were set up by these ancient road builders to help those who would travel after them.

Throughout the ages, God has inspired the use of different kinds of "guidestones" to help point direction for His people through life. As the children of Israel crossed the Jordan, God instructed Joshua to set up twelve stones as a future reminder to the people of God's deliverance. "When your children ask in time to come, saying, 'What do these stones mean?' Then you shall answer them that the waters of the Jordan were cut off before the ark of the covenant of the Lord…and these stones shall be a memorial to the children of Israel forever" (Josh. 4:6–7).

As the prophetic leader of his nation, Samuel set up an "Ebenezer," a "stone of help," to remind the people of the Source of Israel's blessing. "Then Samuel took a stone and set it up between Mizpah and Shen and called its name Ebenezer, saying, 'Thus far the Lord has helped us'" (1 Sam. 7:12). Of course, in the New Testament, our Lord referred to Roman mile markers, these guidestones, when he challenged his followers to go the "second mile" (Matt. 5:41).

If the cry of the Romans in the first century was "all roads lead to Rome," then for those of us involved in growing the church in the 21st century, the cry should be "all roads lead to Jerusalem." The church was birthed in Jerusalem and that is recorded for all posterity in Acts 2. Although it was a brief snapshot in time as it exploded in that city it should, like any founding organization, serve as a model and mentor to us today. It is a sad and tragic day when any nation, any organization, any business, or any church forgets its roots and its underlying foundational beginnings. Pastored by Simon Peter and James, the half brother of our Lord, this first century church impacted its culture and became the "mother church" not only for those local congregations during the first century dispersion but for every local body of baptized believers until this day.

This Jerusalem church set up some guidestones, found in the second chapter of Acts, which should serve today to do exactly what those ancient mile markers did in their day. That is, point the direction in which we should go and warn of the dangers ahead if we should get off the road. We are living in a day when marketing and motivation have replaced ministry and missions in many of the modern church growth movements. More than one popular church growth leader has openly admitted that he finds his mentors not among these first century church leaders but among the CEOs of major corporations. This volume is an appeal for the church to go back to her beginnings and find her mentors among the likes of Simon Peter before the likes of CEO mentors and corporate heads. My appeal is for us to stop thinking it is our job to get the world to start liking the Christian faith. In turn, we need to move the church to stop liking the world and its allures. Yes, to "come out from among them and be separate" (2 Cor. 6:17), as the Lord commanded.

Church growth is big business today. The conversation is of all the new ways of "doing church," of reinventing the church. We are told from many sources that everything has to be "intentional." It seems that there are two things the pastor doesn't need knowledge of any more — theology or church history. No longer is he the dispenser of Biblical doctrine; today he is to be the master storyteller and the one who meets the felt needs of the hearers.

I wonder if Simon Peter would recognize the church today. Whose is the church? Is it ours to "reinvent?" Or, is it still the blood-bought bride of Christ which belongs to Him and Him alone? It seems that we should be more concerned today with "church being" than "church doing" because being always comes before doing. For what we do is determined by who we are and our position in Christ alone.

One church growth leader repeatedly says we should "never criticize what God is blessing." When I hear that, my first thought is who and how do we define what God is blessing and what He is not. Is it simply numbers? Not all crowds are churches. Jeremiah did not have many numbers. Over 50 faithful years he preached with so little tangible results. Was he a failure? God did not think so. And what about the seven churches of Asia in the Revelation? Which of those was the church with the numbers, the one with the crowds? Was it the church at Laodicea which was "wealthy and in need of nothing" (Rev. 3:14–22)? Or, was it the church at Smyrna which was poor and in tribulation (Rev. 2:8–11)? It was the church at Laodicea. And yet to this church our Lord said He wanted to spit them out of His mouth, while He said to the church at Smyrna that they would receive the crown of life. The growing church with the crowds did not please God but the struggling one certainly did. Nickels and noses do not necessarily determine whom God is blessing and whom He is not.

This volume is not a polemic of church growth. So much of the church growth movement is good and refreshing and so culturally relevant. Rather it is a sincere and earnest appeal for the church of the 21st century to rediscover four vital and valuable guidestones which are found in the second chapter of Acts. It is an appeal not to reinvent the church but to rediscover some truths which lead to real revival among the people of God. It is an appeal to not forsake the heart of the New Testament gospel for a New Trendy gospel. Yes, it is a call to "not forsake the ancient landmarks" in our quest to reach a lost and dying generation. Let's hasten on and seek direction from our spiritual forefathers in Jerusalem and learn from the guidestones they left for all of us who would come after them. In authentic church growth the way to go forward is to go back, back to the founding, back to Jerusalem. The journey unfolds on the pages before us with the prayer that it will bring a needed and healthy balance to all that is so good in the church growth movement.

# INTRODUCTION

In a myriad of ways the volume you hold in your hands capsulates my many years of pastoral ministry from the little town of Hobart on the plains of southwestern Oklahoma to the concrete canyons of downtown Dallas. It has been my distinct privilege to be the Lord's undershepherd in four wonderful congregations of believers covering the entire spectrum of pastoral experience. While at the First Baptist Church of Hobart, Oklahoma, I learned that the pastorate is the people business in a very real sense and that life is about relationships. While at the First Baptist Church in Ada, Oklahoma, those good and godly people with a rich pulpit heritage inspired me to become an expository preacher. While serving the First Baptist Church in Fort Lauderdale, Florida, I had the privilege of being on the cutting edge of church growth and for a decade and a half watched God do what few local churches have been blessed to see. Then at the First Baptist Church of Dallas I found anew the stewardship of pastoral authority and the respect of heritage and history.

The American church today is somewhat schizophrenic. While we see some of the largest and most vibrant churches in all of church history, at the same time it seems we are hard-pressed to find many growing, impacting congregations in most of the towns and villages across the land. Thus, the pursuit of "relevance" is the call and cry of the day for many in the modern church growth movement. Os Guinness, in his book, *Prophetic Untimeliness*, reveals a link between our irrelevance and our pursuit of relevance. Guinness warns: "By our uncritical pursuit of relevance we have actually courted irrelevance; by our breathless chase after relevance without a matching commitment to faithfulness, we have become not only unfaithful but irrelevant; by our determined efforts to redefine ourselves in ways that are more compelling to the modern world than are faithful to Christ, we have lost not only our identity but our authority and our relevance. Our crying need is to be faithful as well as relevant." It would do us all well to stop a moment and read that quote once again until it incarnates in our minds. Os Guinness has hit the bulls-eye of the target. Never in church history has the church made such a determined effort to become relevant to a culture; and sadly, in the process, perhaps never in church history has the church become more irrelevant to the lives of the masses than today.

This is certainly not to say there is not much good and healthy in the modern church growth movement. It is asking some very important questions, not the least of which is "what is your purpose in life?" Let's be honest, whether some like the way paraphrased scripture seems to be loosely used in the *Purpose Driven Life* concept, we are hard pressed to go anywhere that we do not encounter men and women whose lives have been enriched, yes transformed, by the truth of the book's pages.

The tragic truth is thousands of churches in America are on life support. They are dying. Many of them are trying to connect with a 21st century world while they refuse to move out of their 1970s church culture. Think about your last trip to your local shopping mall. You walked by store after store, most selling clothes. Clothing has a primary purpose; to cover your body and to keep you warm. What makes you walk into one of those stores? After all, every one of those vendors products fulfill their primary purpose, cover and warmth. But why do you go into some of those stores and stay out of others?

Have you ever stepped into one of those stores and thought you had stepped back a few decades in time? There on the racks were items that a typical adult would not wear today. Instead, there were polyester double-knit suits on mannequins. You saw polyester leisure suits, some bright yellow; others lime green and still others in pastels. The shoe section showcased nothing but those patent leather shoes men were wearing in the 1970s.

That store would be locked in a time warp. They also would soon be having a going out-of-business sale. But down the corridor is a bright, well lit, new store. There you find clothes that are in style, that meet the needs of a changing culture. Meanwhile, the first store manager wonders why people no longer like their consistency. Styles, fabrics and colors change. It doesn't mean the purpose of clothing has changed. It is still to cover the body. But what sold years ago does not attract customers today.

There are many churches in America who are locked in a cultural time warp. Oh, their purpose has not changed. Their message has not changed. But their methods have not changed either and people walk by their "store" in droves. They often do a better job of fulfilling their purpose with the right message. Some of those new stores are barely covering the body with their clothing. But, somewhere along the line some of our churches have become locked into a cultural time warp and people are passing us by even though we have the right message.

The heart-cry of this volume is a call for the church to be cautious not to alter the message of the gospel while trying to incorporate methods that are more conducive to reaching a 21st century world. Methods, like wine skins, should constantly be changing…but not at the expense of neglecting the foundational doctrinal truths of the Word of God and its message of the gospel. My fear is that some elements of the New Trendy gospel message would be unrecognizable to the leaders of the Jerusalem church who passed on to us the authentic New Testament gospel.

As we noted in the foreword, if all roads in the first century led to Rome, all roads in the 21st century lead to Jerusalem when we speak of the church. The church was conceived in the mind of God in the ages past, was gestated in Palestine during the life of Christ and was birthed in Jerusalem where it was empowered by the Holy Spirit. People from all over the known world gathered there for the Feast of Pentecost. As many as one million Jews descended upon the city for this annual celebration. On this particular day 120 believers became the center of attention. Always held 50 days after Passover, the Feast of Pentecost had been observed for 1,500 years. It was designed to celebrate the arrival of the Israelites to Mount Sinai after their deliverance from Egypt. During that feast God had the attention of the city, and ultimately, the world, and through one local body of believers He turned the world upside down. God visited them in the power of His Spirit, Peter stood up and preached a Biblical message, and called the people to repentance and faith, three thousand were converted, and the church was born.

As we place the major emphasis of the modern church growth movement against the emphasis we find in this early church we may be surprised to see how much they are in diametric opposition to each other in four distinct ways. One, the modern church growth movement seems to de-emphasize the place of the Holy Spirit in dynamic church growth. In fact, read many church growth manuals and you will find much more about such things as marketing and motivation than such things as the filling of the Holy Spirit and the functioning of the spiritual gifts of ministry and service. Two, the modern church growth movement seems to de-emphasize Biblical exposition. In many cases it emphatically discourages it. One of the gurus of church growth goes so far as to say it is a distraction to seekers who are in need of story telling to illustrate the meeting of their felt needs. Three, the modern church growth movement seems to de-emphasize doctrinal teaching. One is hard pressed to find much doctrine being taught in many churches. Some even contend that it should be avoided because it can become divisive! Finally, the modern church growth movement has a glaring de-emphasis upon confrontational evangelism. The "go and tell" of the Great Commission has been changed to a polite "come and hear."

What is the answer to these glaring omissions? Remember, when it comes to church growth, all roads lead back to Jerusalem. As we begin to dissect the second chapter of Acts in the pages to follow we will be awakened to see there are four guidestones set up by the early church to point direction for us and to warn of danger as we seek to nurture the growth of a healthy church in our day.

GuideStone #1 reminds us of the importance of **the power of the gospel.** We read in Acts 2 that these early church members were "all filled with the Holy Spirit." Who is teaching about the Holy Spirit and His ministry in and through the believer and in and through the church today? He has become the forgotten member of the Godhead in a quest that majors on marketing and stark pragmatism. Acts 19:2 could be written across the foreheads of many church members in many modern churches today, "We have not so much as heard that there is a Holy Spirit."

GuideStone #2 reminds us of the importance of **the proclamation of the gospel.** Peter stands before the people, opens his "Bible" to the book of Joel, and establishes a Biblical basis for the phenomenon that was happening. He then illustrates his message with two Psalms and preaches his Pentecostal proclamation in a balanced way with "doctrine, reproof, correction, and instruction in righteousness." Who is advocating expository preaching today? Certainly not many of the modern church gurus who speak short messages in narrative form designed to meet felt needs.

GuideStone #3 reminds us of the importance of **the preservation of the gospel.** We read in Acts 2 that these early believers "continued steadfastly in the apostles' doctrine." Who is teaching doctrine today? It is, quite frankly, intentionally avoided in many churches. There are preachers in some pulpits of recognized churches today who know very little of theology or church history and could not tell Athanasius from Augustine. Sociology and psychology take precedent over theology in many churches identified with modern church growth. One must ask what kind of faith is going to be passed on to the next generation? This omission of doctrine is foreign to the New Testament model. Those early believers preserved the gospel by continuing to pass on the doctrine of the apostles.

GuideStone #4 in the second chapter of Acts reminds us of the importance of **the propagation of the gospel.** These early believers had "favor with the people" and they shared their faith with everyone, everywhere they went. Today, many are being discouraged from what one might call confrontational evangelism. Since when has the gospel ceased to be an offense to those who do not believe?

As we move now to revisit these guidestones in depth, the appeal is to a balanced ministry of the gospel. Every

New Testament church should exhibit each of these four guidestones. There are some who are strong on proclamation but have little preservation. Others are big on preservation but with little or no emphasis on propagation. Some make much of the propagation of the gospel but little emphasis is placed on the power of the Holy Spirit in the gospel message. This early church left us four important guidestones upon which to build our churches in the 21st century. Churches that see the blessing of God are those who honor the place and power of the Holy Spirit in their midst, who make much of the Word of God, who preserve their new converts with doctrinal truth, and who continue to exist for those who are in need of a gospel witness beyond their walls.

Yes, the way forward in church growth is to go back. All roads lead back to Jerusalem.

# The power of the gospel

*(Acts 2:1–13)*

A long the road on our journey back to Jerusalem we come to GuideStone #1 left for us by our spiritual forefathers in the early church. It points the direction for the power of the gospel to us and warns of dangers if it is neglected. Tragically, we are seeing a de-emphasis in the modern church of the Holy Spirit's ministry and the part He plays in the revitalization of Christ's church. If this first church was characterized by anything, it was characterized by power. They found their power (*dunamis,* from which we get our word "dynamite") in the personal experience of being "filled with the Holy Spirit" (Acts 2:4). Unfortunately, in many of our modern day churches the statement of Acts 19:2 could be exclaimed by many members,

"We haven't so much as heard that there was a Holy Spirit." This forgotten member of the Godhead is seldom mentioned in a New Trendy type of gospel that seems to de-emphasize the importance of being Spirit-filled or Spirit-led.

The difference in the first century church and 21st century church can be found in two words — influence and power. The early church did not have enough influence with the world to keep Peter out of prison. But they had enough power to pray him out! Today the church seems to pride herself more in the ability to influence people in high places. Go into the studies of large churches' pastors' offices today and you are likely to see pictures with the governor, the mayor or even the President. Influence is the name of the game in much of church life today. But where is this power we read about in the lives of these early believers in Acts who "turned their world upside down?"

In the modern world where self-help overshadows being filled with God's spirit, the Spirit world of the likes of Peter, Paul, Whitfield, Edwards, Carey, Spurgeon, Moody and so many others seems to be disappearing and even replaced by modern motivational gurus with business success principles. "Reinventing" the church has, for some, become more important than "revival" in the church.

As we stop for a moment at this ancient landmark

pointing us to a rediscovery of the church's power, we read these words,

"When the Day of Pentecost had fully come, they were all with one accord in one place. And suddenly there came a sound from heaven, as of a rushing mighty wind, and it filled the whole house where they were sitting. Then there appeared to them divided tongues, as of fire, and one sat upon each of them. And they were all filled with the Holy Spirit and began to speak with other tongues, as the Spirit gave them utterance.

And there were dwelling in Jerusalem Jews, devout men, from every nation under heaven. And when this sound occurred, the multitude came together, and were confused, because everyone heard them speak in his own language. Then they were all amazed and marveled, saying to one another, 'Look, are not all these who speak Galileans? And how is it that we hear, each in our own language in which we were born? Parthians and Medes and Elamites, those dwelling in Mesopotamia, Judea and Cappadocia, Pontus and Asia, Phrygia and Pamphylia, Egypt and the parts of Libya adjoining Cyrene, visitors from Rome, both Jews and proselytes, Cretans and Arabs — we

hear them speaking in our own tongues the wonderful works of God.' So they were all amazed and
perplexed, saying to one another, 'Whatever could
this mean?'

Others mocking said, 'They are full of new
wine'" (Acts 2:1–13).

Note the word *all*. They were *all* together, *all* in one
accord, *all* in one place, and *all* filled. Our spiritual forefathers found their power in two tremendously important
ingredients — unity and unction.

## Unity

The members of the early church found their strength
in participation with one another. They were "with one
accord" (Acts 2:1). They were united and not divided. They
decided to stay together as well as pray together. Unity is
one of the single most important factors in church growth.
We are talking about unity and not uniformity. Cults
emphasize uniformity, while the church emphasizes unity.
The church is the picture of a quartet with each member
singing different parts of the same song but blending
together in perfect harmony.

What was the real phenomenon occurring on the day
the church was born? It was a miracle of sound and sight.
There was a miracle *of sound:* "And suddenly there came a

sound from heaven, as of a rushing mighty wind, and it filled the whole house where they were sitting" (Acts 2:2). The *sound* of the wind was the sign of the Holy Spirit. Earlier Jesus taught in His conversation with Nicodemus, "The wind blows where it wishes, and you hear the sound of it, but cannot tell where it comes from and where it goes. So is everyone who is born of the Spirit" (John 3:8). There was also the miracle of *sight*. "Then there appeared to them divided tongues, as of fire, and one sat upon each of them" (Acts 2:3). There were divided tongues of fire which, like the wind, was the sign of the Holy Spirit. Fire that consumes. Oh how our Lord desires to consume us as His church.

There is plenty of talk in some church circles today about seeing Pentecost repeated. How many times have we heard phrases such as, "They had a Pentecost at such and such church?" If Pentecost is repeated there will be some signs. We will hear the sound of a rushing, mighty wind and see divided, cloven tongues of fire appearing above each head. People will speak in *glossa* (languages) and *dialektos* (dialects). Why are we not seeing this phenomenon in the church today? There is no need for Pentecost to be repeated. It was a one-time event.

The coming of the Holy Spirit to indwell the believers and never to leave them, just like Bethlehem, was a one-time event and never needs to be repeated. It was like Calvary which was a one-time event and never needs to be repeated. Pentecost is the same. At Bethlehem, we see God *with* us. At Calvary, we see God *for* us. At Pentecost, we see God *in* us. For a Christian to pray, "Lord, send the Holy Spirit just like you did on the Day of Pentecost" would be the same as praying, "Lord, send Jesus to Bethlehem to be born of a virgin." He already has. It would be the same as praying, "Lord, send Jesus out to Calvary to die on a cross for our sins." He already has! Pentecost was a one-time event when the Holy Spirit came to indwell the believers, never to leave them and to empower them for service.

Note that the blessing on the Day of Pentecost came "suddenly" (Acts 2:2). It was not obtained through a process of growth or development. No one taught anyone else how to do what happened. It did not evolve out of one's own mental attitudes. It was the sovereign, supernatural gift of the Father upon each person. No one was excluded (see Acts 2:3). It was not manifested by merit. It was the work of God. It came "suddenly," and the effect was that "all of them were filled with the Holy Spirit" (Acts 2:4).

One of the problems of the 21st century is that it has lost its expectancy. It is amazing how many events came about in the early church "suddenly." They seemed to live in anticipation of the unexpected. In Acts 2 the early believers were not waiting until they became worthy. They were praying and waiting, and "suddenly" the Spirit came. Think of the shepherds living in the fields, keeping watch over their flocks at night:

"And behold, an angel of the Lord stood before them, and the glory of the Lord shone around them, and they were greatly afraid. Then the angel said to them, 'Do not be afraid, for behold, I bring you good tidings of great joy which will be to all people. For there is born to you this day in the city of David a Savior, who is Christ the Lord. And this will be the sign to you: You will find a Babe wrapped in swaddling cloths, lying in a manger.'

*Suddenly* there was with the angel a multitude of the heavenly host praising God and saying: 'Glory to God in the highest, and on earth peace, goodwill toward men!'" (Luke 2:9–14, author's italics).

Think of the apostle Paul on the Damascus road. The Bible records:

"Then Saul, still breathing threats and murder against the disciples of the Lord, went to the high priest and asked letters from him to the synagogues of Damascus, so that if he found any who were of the Way, whether men or women, he might bring them bound to Jerusalem. As he journeyed he came near Damascus, and *suddenly* a light shone around him from heaven" (Acts 9:1–3, author's italics).

Think of Silas and Paul in prison at Philippi. The Bible records:

> "But at midnight Paul and Silas were praying and singing hymns to God, and the prisoners were listening to them. *Suddenly* there was a great earthquake, so that the foundations of the prison were shaken; and immediately all the doors were opened and everyone's chains were loosed" (Acts 16:25–26, author's italics).

Oh, the possibility of those of us who live in the realm of expecting the unexpected!

On the day the church was born, the believers were "all with one accord in one place" (Acts 2:1). They sensed a ministry of attendance. They had felt that ministry since earlier in the upper room when Thomas was "not there when Jesus came." Now, they were in their place, "all with one accord in one place." The church today would sense more power if its members lived in anticipation and were all together in one place.

Every layperson in every church has a ministry of attendance. One of the saddest verses in all the Bible is recorded in John 20:24 where the Scripture reveals, "Thomas...was not with the disciples when Jesus came." How urgent it is to be in one's place at the time of worship. I have often wondered where Thomas was that day. Wherever he was was not really the central concern; the point was, he was *not where he should have been when Jesus came.* Like Thomas, we are missing out when we are not fulfilling our ministry of attendance. The Lord brought not only His *presence* into the group that day, but also His *peace.* One never knows when he is not in his place if Jesus will pass by in tremendous power and presence. I am convinced that the actual reason Thomas was not there when Jesus came was the identical reason so many people in so many churches today do not fulfill their ministry of attendance. They simply do not expect Jesus to be there! A large percentage of church members attend as if they were going to some sort of committee meeting, town council meeting, or motivational seminar without any thought that Jesus is actually passing by. Each of us has an awesome responsibility and a "ministry of attendance" at our own local church.

There are so many people in church today who want to "hear" a mighty, rushing wind or "see" cloven tongues of fire. This was an event never to be repeated. I am not claiming that God could not do this again, but I am saying it certainly seems that He has not chosen to manifest Himself in such a way today. God may move dramatically to work in our lives which involves the senses — what we can see, hear, touch, smell, or taste, or, more likely, He will use gentle breezes and whispers. Remember Elijah? The Lord commanded him,

> "Go out, and stand on the mountain before the Lord."

> "And behold, the Lord passed by, and a great and strong wind tore into the mountains and broke the rocks in pieces before the Lord, but the Lord was not in the wind; and after the wind an earthquake, but the Lord was not in the earthquake; and after the earthquake a fire, but the Lord was not in the fire; and after the fire a still small voice" (I Kings 19:11–12).

Elijah was in desperate need to hear from God. There was a mighty wind, but God was not in the wind. There was an earthquake, but God was not in the earthquake. There was a fire, but God was not in the fire. And finally the Bible says, "a gentle whisper, a still small voice."[1] This is generally the way it happens to me, "a still small voice in my heart."

*One of the real characteristics of the first century church was unity.* They were in one accord, in one place. In fact, it is amazing how, as we read through the Book of Acts, they continued to find their strength in participation with each other. They began in Acts 1:14: "These all continued with one accord in prayer and supplication, with the women and Mary the mother of Jesus, and with His brothers." They continued in Acts 2:1: "When the day of Pentecost had fully come, they were all with one accord in one place." After the day of Pentecost the Bible records, "So continuing daily with one accord in the temple, and breaking bread from house to house, they ate their food with gladness and simplicity of heart" (Acts 2:46).

After Peter and John had been arrested, the Bible emphasizes, "So when they heard that, they raised their voice to God with one accord and said: 'Lord, You are God, who made heaven and earth and the sea, and all that is in them'" (Acts 4:24). When deep fear came upon them after the death of Ananias and Sapphira the Bible records, "And through the hands of the apostles many signs and wonders were done among the people. And they were all with one accord in Solomon's Porch" (Acts 5:12). The secret to the growth of the early church was its living together in love and unity.

The most important fact is not what they saw or heard but that they were "all in one accord in one place." They were in one accord, and God met them in that place. Unity, and unction were manifest. They were as different as people in churches today, but God cemented them together and did great and mighty works through them. Look at those in that group. Peter was there. He was so boisterous and the one who denied our Lord before a maiden. Thomas the doubter was present. John and James were in the midst, having been so selfish in wanting to have the number one and number two positions in the Kingdom. There were forgiven adulterers and also tax collectors. You name it, and they were there — Joseph of Arimathea and civic leaders like Nicodemus. They were all different but their secret was they were "all in one accord" in one place. There was power in unity. They found strength in participation with each other.

*Unity was the key to the outpouring of God's Spirit.* This group was so diverse. In fact, it was probably much more diverse than most churches are today. This church did not fish for men like some do today. That is, they didn't "market" their ministry to one certain type of individual in a certain socio-economic group. Some today fish for men with "hooks." They only want to catch one type of fish so they use a lure that only appeals to one certain specimen of fish. This Jerusalem church fished with "nets" and they caught men and women of all types, shapes and sizes. They had the richest of the rich in Joseph of Arimathea and the poorest of the poor in the widow. Yet, they were "all in one accord." There seemed to be no petty bickering, no silly jealousy. So many churches today are filled with people who are backbiting and murmuring. Many of us ought to stop worrying about getting a blessing and start worrying about being a blessing. The secret of this Jerusalem church was participation. They found their strength in participation with one another. This is the real key to a great church in the eyes of God. Unity was the theme. They were "all in one accord in one place."

## Unction

They not only found their power in participation with one another, but in participation with God. *"All* of them were filled with the Holy Spirit" (Acts 2:4, author's italics). Not some of them but all of them! They had been baptized, indwelt, and sealed by the Holy Spirit; now they were filled by Him. The emphasis in Acts 2 is on the filling of the Holy Spirit. This puts us under the spotlight of the principle of "being before doing," for what we do is always determined by who we are and what we are. While baptism with the Holy Spirit is a once-and-for-all encounter, the filling of the Holy Spirit is to be repeated over and over again. This is what makes a church great in the eyes of God — a Spirit-filled membership where Jesus is the Lord of every life. At conversion we have the Holy Spirit. When we are filled, the Holy Spirit has us!

The work of the Holy Spirit in our lives involves several factors. It involves the *baptism with the Holy Spirit.* First Corinthians 12:13 says: "For by one Spirit we were all baptized into one body — whether Jews or Greeks, whether slaves or free — and have all been made to drink into one Spirit."

There is also the *indwelling of the Holy Spirit.* Romans 8:9 says: "But you are not in the flesh but in the Spirit, if indeed the Spirit of God dwells in you. Now if anyone does not have the Spirit of Christ, he is not His." Then there is the *sealing of the Holy Spirit.* Ephesians 1:13–14 states: "In Him you also trusted, after you heard the word of truth, the gospel of your salvation; in whom also, having believed, you were sealed with the Holy Spirit of promise, who is the guarantee of our inheritance until the redemption of the purchased possession, to the praise of His glory."

Next comes the *filling of the Holy Spirit* found in Ephesians 5:18: "And do not be drunk with wine, in which is dissipation; but be filled with the Spirit." The filling is conditional upon our surrender to Jesus as Lord.

There is also the *anointing of the Holy Spirit.* At the Lord's baptism, the Holy Spirit anointed Him. The anointing is a special touch for a special task. Thank God for the anointing! No preacher ought to preach without asking God for "fresh oil" — the anointing. No singer ought to sing without asking God for the anointing. No teacher ought to teach the Bible without asking God for the anointing.

What is the command of the Bible in regards to the Holy Spirit? Is it to be *baptized* with the Holy Spirit? No! There is not one command in Scripture to be baptized with the Holy Spirit. In fact, if we are saved, the Bible teaches us we have already been baptized with the Holy Spirit. Are we commanded to be *indwelt* by the Holy Spirit? No! Is the command, then, to be *sealed* with the Holy Spirit? Again, the answer is no. The command of Scripture in regards to the Holy Spirit is to "be filled with the Spirit" (Eph. 5:18).

The filling of the Holy Spirit is a command. The word translated into the English *be filled* is the word *plerousthe* in the original language. Every verb has a number, tense, voice, and mood. When we look at this word *be filled* in Ephesians 5:18, we find that the number is plural. The tense is present, continuous action. The voice is passive, meaning that the subject doesn't act. It is acted upon. The mood is imperative. There is no option. Therefore, properly translated, the command to be filled in Ephesians 5:18 is saying, "all of you must always be being filled with the Holy Spirit."

What makes a church great in the eyes of God? GuideStone #1 is the power of the gospel. This involves *unity* (participation with each other) and *unction* (participation with God).

What actually happened in Acts 2? It was a phenomenon! They spoke in other languages. Is this happening today? What transpired? It is important to grasp what the Bible really reveals about this incredible event. After all, if our experience does not match the Word of God, it is not valid. As we come before God's Word, we should try to strip away any preconceived prejudices and simply want to know, "What does the Bible say about this happening?"

Some argue, "I don't care what the Bible says. I know what I have experienced." They are subjective, believing more in their feelings than the inspired, written Word of God. In this study we are not preoccupied with the "charismatic" view. It generally claims that if you are really filled with the Holy Spirit, the evidence is you will speak in tongues, since for most charismatics that is a sign of the filling. Nor are we interested in what the charisphobiac declares. He usually argues it is all of the devil, which puts him in a terrible position. We want to know, "What does God's Word say?" How can we "rightly divide the word of truth" and understand what is actually said about this phenomenal event? Like those men and women who were there that day, we ask, "Whatever could this mean?" (Acts 2:12). With an open Bible, the answer is extremely plain. We never have to be afraid of what the Bible declares, regardless of whether or not it fits our preconceived ideas. The bottom line is the Word of God, not my experience or my pet ideas.

Many people cry, "I've had a Pentecostal experience." Well, if so, that experience will line up and measure up with Scripture. We should look at every experience we have through the Word of God and test its validity. After all, John exhorts us to "test the spirits, whether they are from God, because many false prophets have gone out into the world" (1 John 4:1). We do not have to be afraid of what the Word of God says because the Word is profitable.

In first century Palestine the spoken language was Aramaic, and the written language was Greek. Alexander the Great had conquered the known world, and the Greek language had spread as a universal language. Therefore, when the New Testament was written, it was written in the Greek language. Our task is to find the most ancient Greek manuscripts we can and go back as close to the original autographs as possible. We should want to study the language in which Luke wrote as he penned the word in the book of Acts. The Greek word in Acts 2:4, which is translated *tongues,* is the word *glossa.* It means language. It means *known* language. In fact, we receive our English word *glossary* from this Greek word. These were languages foreign to the speaker which he had never heard, but by which he was supernaturally empowered to speak as a result of the Holy Spirit. The phenomenon happened with the Jews at Pentecost in Acts 2. It happened again with the disciples of John the Baptist at Ephesus in Acts 19. Each time the word *glossa* is used, Jews were present, and unbelieving Jews were in the background.

What happened at Pentecost was that these were all languages unknown to the speakers and spoken at that particular time in demonstration of the entrance of the age of grace.

They were not unknown languages. In fact, we do not read in the New Testament about an "unknown tongue." You might ask, "What about 1 Corinthians 14:2?" In the King James version, this Scripture says, "For he that speaketh in an *"unknown"* tongue speaketh not unto men, but unto God: for no man understandeth him; howbeit in the spirit he speaketh mysteries." If you will read carefully, the word *unknown* is in italics in our English Bibles, indicating that it is not found in the Greek manuscripts but inserted by translators. *The New King James Version* omits the word *unknown,* and rightly so. These languages spoken on the Day of Pentecost were *known* dialects. Everyone heard them speaking in their own language (Acts 2:8).

It is interesting that this same word *glossa* used in Acts 2:4 is also found in Revelation 5:9. In this picture of heaven, we read these words:

"And they sang a new song, saying:

'You are worthy to take the scroll,

And to open its seals;

For You were slain,

And have redeemed us to God by

Your blood

Out of every tribe and *tongue* and people

and nation'" (author's italics).

It is also found in Revelation 7:9:

"After these things I looked, and behold, a great multitude which no one could number, of all nations, tribes, peoples, and *tongues*, standing before the throne and before the Lamb, clothed with white robes, with palm branches in their hands" (author's italics).

The word means language. It is linguistic and not some incoherent babbling.

What is the difference between the words which are translated in the English word *tongue* in Acts 2:4 and the words translated *language* in Acts 2:6, 8? In verse 4 the word is *glossa,* and in verses 6 and 8 the word is *dialektos.* Verse 8 is translated by the English word *tongue* in the King James Version, but properly translated in *The New King James Version* as *language.* This latter word means *dialect.*[2] What we have is the word for *language* in Acts 2:4 and the word for *dialect* in Acts 2:6, 8.

So what do we mean? What happened? People gathered from all over the known world for the Feast of Pentecost. There were between 12 and 17 (depending on the translation) different languages represented at that feast on that particular day. The miracle was in the hearing. They heard not just in their own language, but in the dialect which they spoke! For example, in First Baptist, Fort Lauderdale, we had a man from Alabama who was a good friend of a man from Brooklyn, who were both friends of a man from London, England. They all spoke English, but each of their dialects was as different as daylight and dark!

What happened on the Day of Pentecost were known languages spoken in dialects. There is no possibility that Acts 2 refers to any type of unknown gibberish. This was not merely a bunch of different syllables all thrown together like so many people try to teach others today. It passed the test of linguistics. These were known languages of the day, and the miracle was not in the speaking as much as it was in the hearing. No one was teaching anyone else how to speak it. They were hearing it not only in their own language, but the miracle was they heard it in their own dialect!

It is intriguing to pay attention to those who were assembled there that day. "And there were dwelling in Jerusalem Jews, devout men, from every nation under heaven" (Acts 2:5). This tongue was a sign/gift to the Jewish nation. This is what Paul means in 1 Corinthians 14:21–22:

"In the law it is written: 'With men of other tongues and other lips I will speak to this people; And yet, for all that, they will not hear Me,' says the Lord."

Therefore tongues are for a sign, not to those who believe but to unbelievers; but prophesying is not for unbelievers but for those who believe.

"*This people*" refers to the Jews. It was a sign to the unbelievers, who were present whenever tongues occurred in the New Testament. It consisted of known languages and was addressed to God in praise. They did not preach the gospel in tongues in Acts 2; they spoke about the wonderful works of God (Acts 2:11). After grabbing the attention of the crowd, Peter stood up and preached a gospel sermon in the known language of the day. An interpreter was not needed in this phenomenon in Acts 2.

The result was amazing. "Then they were all amazed and marveled, saying to one another, "Look, are not all these who speak Galileans?' " (Acts 2:7). People began to ask, "How can these men speak these different *glossa* and *dialektos* (languages and dialects)? They are neither educated nor traveled. They are not from the universities or the seminaries. Look at them! They are rough, crude, callous-handed Galilean fishermen. How is it that when they speak we hear in our language of the wonderful works of God?" We must remember that this event occurred long before the days of the art of linguistics. It was difficult to learn foreign languages in the first century world. One had to live in a particular country for a considerable period of time. And yet, these Galileans, untrained and unlearned, were speaking in foreign languages and dialects about the wonderful works of God. The miracle was not just in the speaking, but it was in the hearing.

Where is the miracle at Pentecost being repeated today? Some preach we need another Pentecost, so they go to an altar, speak a bunch of unintelligible syllables, perhaps jump up and down, and claim they have had the "Pentecostal experience." It is plain what will happen if you have a Pentecostal experience; you will hear the sound of a rushing wind, see cloven tongues of fire, and speak in known languages and dialects which you have never heard, and people will hear in their native language without needing an interpreter! Where is this happening today?

What happened here? Why doesn't it seem to be happening anymore? Some insist it is happening. But the truth is that it is not happening as it did on the Day of Pentecost, manifested with wind, fire, and languages. What was transpiring here? This was the beginning of a new dispensation of the Holy Spirit, the age of grace. What did God do at the beginning of each new dispensation? He introduced it with wonders, signs and miracles which were not necessarily ever repeated.

This is true all through the Word of God. For example, when God created the earth, all matter, He did it with wonders and signs and miracles. He spoke, and it came into being. But since the early chapters of Genesis, not one single atom of matter has been created out of nothing. The same is true when God began the dispensation of the Law. It was ushered in with wonders and signs and miracles which have not been repeated. There was the parting of the Red Sea and the parting of the Jordan. There was a cloud by day and a pillar of fire by night, which led the children of Israel. There was also the manna falling from heaven. This is not to deny that God could do any of these miracles again, but He obviously does not work in exactly that manner today. There is only one dispensation remaining. It will come at the end of this age of grace with the second coming of our Lord Jesus Christ and will be accompanied by signs, wonders, and miracles that the world has yet to see.[3]

God can do whatever He wants — except violate His own will and character. He can create something out of nothing anytime He desires. He can part an ocean and rain down manna from heaven. But He is not doing such today as He did at the beginning of these dispensations. This certainly does not imply that He is any less of a God. He is always the same — yesterday, today and forever.

Pentecost marked the beginning of the church age, the age of the Holy Spirit, the age of grace. And like other dispensations, it was accompanied with signs, wonders, and miracles (rushing, mighty winds and flaming tongues of fire, as well as *glossa* and *dialektos* spoken by unlearned men).

As the Book of Acts continues, we will see this third sign of speaking in languages, when the gospel is preached for the Gentiles at the home of Cornelius, a Roman centurion at Caesarea (Acts 10). Describing this event, Peter says, "If therefore God gave them the *same gift* as He gave us when we believed on the Lord Jesus Christ, who was I that I could withstand God?" (Acts 11:17 author's italics). It emphasized that it was the "same gift." What happened in Acts 10 at Caesarea was the same thing that happened at Pentecost. That is, it was *glossa* and *dialektos!*

We see the identical thing again in Acts 19 when the gospel is preached at Ephesus, the great capital city of the Roman province of Asia. They magnified the Lord with *glossa* — known languages. It was not unintelligible babbling. This is not what *we think* happened at Pentecost, Caesarea, and Ephesus; it is what the Bible clearly teaches when we study what it actually says. All of us should be concerned more about what God's Word says than what someone else says about God's Word or some experience that may not measure alongside God's Word.

In 1 Corinthians 13:8, Paul says *glossa* shall cease. That is in and of itself. Some believe that like signs, which accompanied the Mosaic dispensation and the age of grace, they have not been seen again. When Paul said in 1 Corinthians 13 that knowledge and prophecy would cease, he used the word *katargeo,* which means to make idle, inoperative. It is the same word employed in 1 Corinthians 13:11, where the Bible states we "put away childish things." However, when Paul, in the same context states that *glossa* will cease, he uses the word *pausontai* which means automatically ceased of themselves. The Bible prophesied that there was coming a time when these gifts would cease. Prophecy and knowledge would simply cease, but tongues would cease *in and of themselves.* We cannot argue this. What we can argue is when this time was or will be. Many believe that such gifts as *glossa* and *dialektos* ceased with the completion of the New Testament.

We now have the complete revelation of God (the Bible), which makes fragmentary revelation pointless. Perhaps this is what Paul refers to in 1 Corinthians 13:10, when he writes, "But when that which is perfect has come, then that which is in part will be done away." What is perfect? It is the inerrant, infallible Word of the living God. Then what does he mean when he declares that "the imperfect disappears" in the last part of verse 10? These gifts belonged to the infancy of the church, and as the church matured they were no longer needed. This is the reason for the next verse, which goes, "When I was a child, ...I thought like a child, I understood like a child. When I became a man, I put away childish things" (1 Cor. 13:11).

Did this particular sign/gift cease? It should be noted that one of Paul's earliest epistles was the first epistle written to the Corinthian church in or around 55 A.D. It was here, 1 Corinthians 12–14, that he spoke regarding *glossa* and stated in 1 Corinthians 13:8 that *glossa* would cease. After writing this epistle, Paul wrote the Roman letter, the marvelous doctrinal treatise of the Christian faith, and tongues were never mentioned. After Paul wrote that epistle, he penned 2 Corinthians, and again tongues were never mentioned. After Paul wrote I Corinthians, the sign of tongues is not mentioned again. Then he wrote Ephesians, the cyclical letter to the church of Asia, and once again there is not one reference to *glossa*. After Paul wrote 1 Corinthians, he wrote Colossians, 1 Thessalonians, 2 Thessalonians, 1 Timothy, 2 Timothy, Titus and Philemon. In all these books not one word is mentioned about these *glossa* or *dialektos*. Why? Many believe it is as Paul wrote in 1 Corinthians 13:8 that *glossa* has ceased.[4]

What is my point? If tongues are as important as certain people attempt to make them to be today, they would have found their place in the letters to the various first-century churches. The only church to which the subject was addressed during the early days of the church age was to a church that was carnal and immature (see 1 Cor. 3). Others claim it is their prayer language. If it were as important as many people try to make it, when the disciples asked the Lord, "Lord, teach us to pray" (Luke 11:1), Jesus would surely have mentioned it.

Ironically, men throughout this age of grace who have been the most mightily used of God never spoke in *glossa* and *dialektos*. They follow the likes of Augustine, Savonarola, Wycliffe, Luther, Calvin, Wesley, Finney, Moody, Spurgeon, Sunday, Graham, and the list continues.

What is the phenomenon of Pentecost that needs to be repeated? Is it the wind? Is it the flaming fire? Is it the *glossa* and *dialektos?* No! It is the filling! All through Acts we read repeatedly that they were filled with the Holy Spirit. That is what we need — the filling of God's Holy Spirit. *At conversion we have the Holy Spirit. At the filling He has us!* And what happened? As they spoke in these other languages and dialects, the people heard them speaking in their own language and dialect. They spoke of the amazing wonders of God and certainly got the attention of the crowd. These tongues did not save a soul; they were attention getters. Three thousand people were saved, and the church was born when the preacher, Simon Peter, stood and preached the Lord Jesus Christ.

Revival comes through the power of the gospel in the filling of His Holy Spirit. But what exactly is the real proof of being filled with God's Holy Spirit? The proof is evidenced in Ephesians 5:19–21. We will recall that the command of God is found in Ephesians 5:18, "be filled with the Spirit." The following verse will present the *inward* evidence. That is, how will *you* know? There will be a song in your heart!

The next verse gives us the *upward* evidence. That is, how will *God* know? Of course God knows everything, but the evidence is in thankfulness. We will have a heart full of thanksgiving and praise. The *outward* evidence is in the following verse. How will *others* know? By our spirit of submission one to another.

## Inward evidence

What is the inward evidence that one is being filled with the Holy Spirit? If God's command is in Ephesians 5:18, the inward evidence is in Ephesians 5:19, "speaking to one another in psalms and hymns and spiritual songs, singing and making melody in your heart to the Lord." What is the evidence? It is singing, even if you can't carry a tune in a bucket. This is the inward evidence of the fullness of God's Holy Spirit. We cannot stay filled with the Holy Spirit without singing. In the original text there is no period after verse 18. This is where we find the difference in Christianity and other world religions. If you look at the followers of Buddha they may have their impressive temples, but they have no song in their hearts. The Hindus may have their mantras, but they have no song in their hearts. Islam may pride itself in its perceived morality but it has no song in its heart. When we are filled with the Holy Spirit, one of the sure proofs is joy. We are joyful inside. I love the title of that old song, "With a Song in My Heart." Even though we may be like Paul and Silas in a Philippian jail at midnight, we cannot help but sing. This is the *inward* evidence of a life that is filled with the Spirit of God.

Note where this inward evidence is manifested — "in your heart" (Eph. 5:19). I am so thankful that the instrument is the heart and not the vocal chords. I often sing in my car when the windows are rolled up. I cannot make melody on an instrument. I cannot make melody with my vocal chords, but I certainly can in my heart!

To whom is this inward evidence directed? "To the Lord" (Eph. 5:19). The Holy Spirit is in the world to uplift and glorify the Lord Jesus. Music is not primarily designed by God to be a tool of evangelism. In other words, Christian music should be the result of a Spirit-filled life that is pointed to God. It is not intended for the world. It is rather unfortunate that many Christian singers today dedicate their songs to the world with the world's beat and the world's vernacular.

How is the inward evidence to be experienced? "Speaking to yourselves in psalms and hymns and spiritual songs, singing and making melody in your heart to the Lord" (Eph. 5:19, KJV). Note that it is making "melody" and not rhythm or harmony. Bill Gothard points out that rhythm appeals to the body, harmony to the soul, but melody is what appeals to the spirit. Think about it. Whichever you find predominant in music is where you will discover its intended appeal. I believe the rhythm of *rock* music appeals to the flesh. The sentimental harmony music appeals to the soul, the self-life. We remember such groups as the Carpenters and all their harmony and love songs. Melody is what appeals to the spirit. We make melody in our hearts to the Lord. Yes, the inward evidence of the filling of God's Holy Spirit is a song in one's heart. If one wants to know if he or she is being filled with the Spirit of God, this should be the first characteristic.

## Upward evidence

There is also an upward evidence of the filling of God's Holy Spirit, "giving thanks always for all things to God the Father in the name of our Lord Jesus Christ" (Eph. 5:20). Again, pay attention to whom this thanksgiving is directed —"to God" (Eph. 5:20). When we begin to recognize God as the Source of everything, and we allow His Spirit to fill us, we will commence giving thanks always for all things unto God and the Father in the name of our Lord Jesus Christ.

We are to offer this upward evidence "always" (Eph. 5:20).

One person chimes in, "But you don't know my problem." Another complains, "But you don't know my wife." Another says, "But you don't know my situation on the job." But the verse says, "always." We are challenged to be thankful at all times because that attitude shows that God is in control. Paul expressed it in these words, "Give thanks in all circumstances, for this is God's will for you in Christ Jesus." If we are looking for a starting point toward finding God's will, that is precisely the place to start. There is an *inward* evidence and an *upward* evidence to the filling of God's Holy Spirit. And notice for what we are to be thankful—"all things" (Eph. 5:20). Some are only thankful after they receive a blessing. We land a new job, and we pray, "Lord, thank you." We recover from a sickness, and we praise, "Lord, thank you." But the evidence of the filling of God's Holy Spirit is that we are thankful in *all things.* This means that we must be thankful not only after our blessings, but before a blessing, in anticipation of the victory we have awareness that it will come.

Being thankful also means we are to be thankful, not merely after and before, but even in the midst of the storms of life. Jonah certainly found this truth to be liberating when he pledged,

"But I will sacrifice to You
With the voice of thanksgiving;
I will pay what I have vowed.
Salvation is of the LORD" (Jonah 2:9).

God appreciated that prayer of thanksgiving so much he had the fish regurgitate Jonah onto the shore. Thanksgiving, this *upward* evidence of the filling of God's Spirit, has a liberating, freeing effect. We cannot stay filled with the Holy Spirit without giving thanks always unto God for all things.

## Outward evidence

There is not only an *inward* and an *upward* evidence, but there is also an *outward* evidence of the filling of the Holy Spirit. Paul continued, "submitting to one another in the fear of God" (Eph. 5:21). What is this outward evidence? It is submission. We are each to esteem the others better than ourselves. People are not sure we are filled with the Holy Spirit by our speech or the terminology we use, but the outward evidence is in our relationship with other people. Christ, of course, is our example. We remember in the upper room on the eve of His death, having instituted the Lord's Supper, how He washed His disciples' feet in a spirit of condescension. Jesus was teaching all that the greatest man is one who uses his authority to build up his people and not like the Pharisee to build himself up. The only means of showing this outward evidence to others is by being filled with the Holy Spirit.

We are to submit to "one another." This is certainly evidence of the Spirit-filled life. Here is the solution to mountains of our problems. To solve difficulties in relationships, we must come to the knowledge of the truth about ourselves. If we are filled with the Holy Spirit we readily recognize that we have nothing to boast about. A person filled with the Holy Spirit is apt to listen and learn. The Holy Spirit helps us to realize we are members of one body, and therefore, our body functions as we submit ourselves to one another. This spirit of *unity* and *unction* is the greatest factor in church growth.

It is also intriguing to see that this outward evidence is to be performed "in the fear of God" (Eph. 5:21). This is not just some phrase tacked onto the end of a verse. We are to be submissive to one another, not because it is expedient, but because we fear God. We fear God, not so much in the sense that we fear Him by being physically afraid, but in the sense that we fear disappointing or grieving Him.

When I was in high school, I obeyed my father. My curfew was earlier than most of my high school friends. My dad always wanted to know where I was and when I was coming home. I obeyed him during those years, because I feared him, not so much that I feared him physically, but

I feared disappointing him. This is what, I suppose, bothered me the most. Why should we live in submission one to another? Because of the fear of God. Could there be anything more terrifying than to realize that we were disappointing the One who loved us so much that He gave Himself for us?

The outward evidence that one is being filled with the Holy Spirit is this mutual submission — one to another. In the Ephesian letter, Paul goes on to illustrate verse 21 in three ways. The next series of verses illustrates this submission regarding the husband/wife relationship. The following verses illustrate this submission in relationship to the parent and child. And finally, to the employer and employee.

Thus, what is the proof that one is genuinely being filled with God's Holy Spirit? Is it a certain, assigned gift, or a certain terminology, or a certain miracle? No! The real proof that one is being filled with the Holy Spirit is found in the context of its command. There is an inward evidence, *a song in one's heart.* There is an upward evidence, *a spirit of thanksgiving.* And there is an outward evidence, *submitting ourselves one to another.* We will never see genuine revival until each of us comes to this element of participation, not only with others in *unity,* but with God in *unction,* the filling of God's Holy Spirit. This is the church member's most pressing need in these last days of church history.

Untold numbers of members in churches today try to give out when they have never taken in. Jesus declared, "He that believes in me as the Scripture has said, out of his belly will flow rivers of living water." There are two kinds of wells — surface wells and artesian wells. A surface well is not very deep.

When I was a small child, I used to visit my great-uncle who ran a country store nine miles outside of Pikeville, Tennessee, on the side of a mountain. I was a city boy and quite fascinated by that lifestyle. They had an old water pump outside the back door of their house. He would go out and pour a little water from the Mason jar into the pump, thus "priming" the pump, and then he would pump, pump, pump, until the water started flowing. As long as he pumped, it would flow, but as soon as he stopped so would the water. And one always had to remember to fill the jar, because it would have to be primed again. Have you ever known any church members like that? If you want them to serve the Lord Jesus, you have to prime the pump. So many try to enlist workers by begging and pleading and stroking. Why? Because those people are shallow like that surface well.

However, there is another kind of well that we call an artesian well. It goes down deep into the ground until it hits an underground stream or river. You don't have to pump an artesian well, all you have to do is tap into it, and it flows and flows. I hope you have known believers like that. Those church members are not complaining, "I've been here six months, and nobody has come to see me!" They are insisting, "Is there anyone I can go and visit?" These people are not carping, "No one spoke to me today!" They pick out people and make a point of speaking to them first. What is the difference? Some want to be served while others want to serve. Some are shallow, while some have tapped into the river of life and are being filled with God's Holy Spirit.

The church will be revived again when more and more of its people experience first-hand the filling of the Holy Spirit in their lives through confession of sin and a total abandonment to Jesus Christ as Lord. The early church found their strength *in participation,* not only with each other, but with God: They were "all filled with the Holy Spirit."

In the midst of a world of modern church growth principles which seldom, if ever, mentions the importance and power of the Holy Spirit it behooves us to remember that all roads lead to Jerusalem. And along that road we come to GuideStone #1 — the power of the gospel. Apart from the power of the Holy Spirit we can never make an impact upon our world. It is the power of the Holy Spirit that gives us unity and unction in the life of the church. Otherwise, our meetings are nothing different from a myriad of other self-help groups and organizations built upon marketing and motivation that produce a false sense of hope achieved through some type of pumped-up mental attitude.

It is the Holy Spirit Himself who empowers His church to make a difference in the world. The Jerusalem church was solely dependent upon the work of the Holy Spirit in their midst. When we read these accounts in Acts we see over and over the necessity of Holy Spirit power. Shouldn't we find it amazing and alarming that this is such an item of de-emphasis in so much of the modern church growth movement? It was through Holy Spirit power that this early church challenged kings and rulers and took the gospel to uncharted territories and hostile environs. Thousands of these early Spirit-filled believers met horrifying martyrs' deaths…all empowered by God's Spirit. And the Bible says "the world was not worthy of them." They turned their world upside down. They left us some guidestones along the journey back to Jerusalem to point direction for us and warn of dangers ahead. At GuideStone #1, we learn there is a difference between influence and power and come to appreciate and hopefully, appropriate the power of the gospel.

# The proclamation of the gospel

*(Acts 2:14–40)*

Along our journey on the road back to Jerusalem we now come to GuideStone #2 left for us by our spiritual forefathers in the early church. It points us in the direction of the proclamation of the gospel and warns us about preaching a message that is void of the gospel itself. Tragically, the call of modern church growth has with it a de-emphasis on expository preaching in its quest to "relate" to felt needs. At Pentecost Simon Peter stood up, opened his scroll to the book of Joel, illustrated his text with two of the Psalms and established a Biblical basis for the phenomenon that was Pentecost.

One of the subtle dangers of some modern church growth techniques lies in an actual, and I am sure unconscious, abandonment of the gospel itself. This should bring us to a foundational question — What is the gospel? Of course, the place to begin to answer this question is in the Bible. The gospel message is not just "good news" to give you a purpose or to make you feel better about yourself. An understanding of the gospel begins with an awareness that man is a sinner in rebellion against God (Rom. 3:23; 5:1–12). While man may be looking for some religious aspect in life, the truth is he does not seek for God or even desire Him according to Romans 3:10–18. Thus man is under the wrath of God (Rom. 1:18) and he faces a future judgment (Heb. 9:27). He is not sick spiritually; he is dead in his trespasses and sin. He is destined, without Christ, to die and spend eternity in hell (Rev. 20:11–15). He can do nothing to redeem himself in the eyes of God (Titus 3:5). So the Lord Jesus Christ out of His marvelous grace came to earth, clothed Himself in human flesh and lived a perfect life among us. He died in our place on the cross taking our sin in His own body and satisfying God's wrath (Rom. 5:8; Heb. 2:17). He arose from the dead in order that we could be saved from our sin and have His own righteousness imputed to us (Rom. 4). While this is all the gift of God's grace we obtain it by placing our faith in Christ alone (Eph. 2:8–10). That is the gospel we are called to proclaim!

However, to hear the "good news" being proclaimed in many churches today is a "different gospel." We are being told that if we just come to Christ, He will meet all our felt needs and that in turn will give us fulfillment in life. Thus, our search for a life of happiness will be over. Eureka! But this is a different gospel from the one the Jerusalem hearers heard from the first century preachers.

The seeker sensitive gospel has a problem at its very roots. It has a flawed anthropology about it. It sees the problem with the lost man as one of being turned off only by the methodology of out-of-date church models and sees the "seeker" actually as a friend of God. Oswald Chambers, the great devotionalist, warned us long ago saying, "We must never confuse our desire for people to accept the gospel with creating a gospel that is acceptable to people."

We must be careful not to confuse this vital issue. I fear that some, in a legitimate concern for people to accept the gospel, have in turn confused the New Testament gospel for a sort of New Trendy gospel which is more concerned with being acceptable to people than to the Lord Himself. The New Testament gospel is a call to self-denial. The New Trendy gospel is a call to self-fulfillment. The New Testament gospel focuses on God's purpose of redemption of man. The New Trendy gospel focuses on man's purpose for happiness in life. The New Testament gospel is about the cross. The New Trendy gospel even removes the cross from its buildings in some places. Prophetically warning us decades ago about these trends, A.W. Tozer put it like this — "If I see aright, the cross of popular evangelicalism is not the cross of the New Testament. It is, rather, a new bright ornament upon the bosom of a self-assured and carnal Christianity. The old cross slew men; the new cross entertains them. The old cross condemned; the new cross amuses. The old cross destroyed confidence in the flesh; the new cross encourages it."

Perhaps of all the ancient landmarks, the most obvious difference in the Jerusalem church and the modern church is in the emphasis, or lack thereof, of the proclamation of the gospel message. Biblical exposition is fast becoming a lost art in contemporary preaching. True exegesis and exposition has given way to topical, narrative, and felt need appeals. More than one influential voice in evangelicalism today is proclaiming that the age of expository preaching has past. Messages designed to reach secular hearers with superficial Biblical truth have taken its place. After all, if you just avoid the Biblical text then you can also avoid all those sticky and somewhat embarrassing issues that Biblical truth has a way of confronting.

Pastors are receiving plenty of counsel in our day about how they should preach. Here is a quotation from a famous pulpiteer: "Preachers who pick out texts from the Bible and then proceed to give the historical settings and the primary meanings in the context are grossly misusing the Bible. Could any procedure be more surely predestined to dullness and futility? One out of a hundred people in your congregation doesn't care what Moses or Isaiah or Paul or John meant in those verses spoken 2,000 years ago. Let the sermon start with thinking about the hearer's needs, and then let the whole sermon be organized around the constructive endeavor to meet those felt needs. This is good sense and good psychology." This is what young preachers are hearing today from many sides. But, the above quotation is more than 50 years old and is from Harry Emerson Fosdick, arguably the most liberal preacher of the first half of the 20th century. Fifty years ago this theological liberal counseled his generation in the same way many modern "conservative" evangelicals are being counseled today. Should this not alarm us about what we are hearing today? This approach to preaching led to the decline and dying state of many mainline denominations. It did not work in the long run then and will not today.

We turn our attention now to Simon Peter's Pentecostal proclamation, GuideStone #2. He "preached the word" to the people and the results were not only apparent, they were abiding. Luke, records the event for all posterity as follows:

"But Peter, standing up with the eleven, raised his voice and said to them, 'Men of Judea and all who dwell in Jerusalem, let this be known to you, and heed my words. For these are not drunk, as you suppose, since it is only the third hour of the day. But this is what was spoken by the prophet Joel:

> And it shall come to pass in the last days,
> says God,
> That I will pour out of My Spirit on all flesh;
> Your sons and your daughters shall prophesy,
> Your young men shall see visions,
> Your old men shall dream dreams.
> And on My menservants and on
> My maidservants
> I will pour out My Spirit in those days;
> And they shall prophesy.
> I will show wonders in heaven above
> And signs in the earth beneath:
> Blood and fire and vapor of smoke.
> The sun shall be turned into darkness,
> And the moon into blood,
> Before the coming of the great and awesome
> day of the LORD.

And it shall come to pass
That whoever calls on the name of the LORD
Shall be saved.'

"Men of Israel, hear these words: Jesus of Nazareth, a Man attested by God to you by miracles, wonders, and signs which God did through Him in your midst, as you yourselves also know — Him, being delivered by the determined purpose and foreknowledge of God, you have taken by lawless hands, have crucified, and put to death; whom God raised up, having loosed the pains of death, because it was not possible that He should be held by it. For David says concerning Him:

'I foresaw the LORD always before my face,
For He is at my right hand, that I may not
be shaken.
Therefore my heart rejoiced, and my tongue
was glad;
Moreover my flesh also will rest in hope.
For You will not leave my soul in Hades,
Nor will You allow Your Holy One to
see corruption.
You have made known to me the ways of life;
You will make me full of joy in Your presence.'"

"Men and brethren, let me speak freely to you of the patriarch David, that he is both dead and buried, and his tomb is with us to this day.

Therefore, being a prophet, and knowing that God had sworn with an oath to him that of the fruit of his body, according to the flesh, He would raise up the Christ to sit on his throne,he, foreseeing this, spoke concerning the resurrection of the Christ, that His soul was not left in Hades, nor did His flesh see corruption. This Jesus God has raised up, of which we are all witnesses. Therefore being exalted to the right hand of God, and having received from the Father the promise of the Holy Spirit, He poured out this which you now see and hear.

> For David did not ascend into the heavens, but he says himself:
> "The LORD said to my Lord,
> 'Sit at My right hand,
> Till I make Your enemies Your footstool.'"

"Therefore let all the house of Israel know assuredly that God has made this Jesus, whom you crucified, both Lord and Christ."

Now when they heard this, they were cut to the heart, and said to Peter and the rest of the apostles, 'Men and brethren, what shall we do?'

"Then Peter said to them, 'Repent, and let every one of you be baptized in the name of Jesus Christ for the remission of sins; and you shall receive the gift of the Holy Spirit. For the promise is to you and to your children, and to all who are afar off, as many as the Lord our God will call.' "

And with many other words he testified and exhorted them, saying, 'Be saved from this perverse generation' " Acts 2:14–40.

Every believer who is halfway conversant with the New Testament will recall the transformation of Simon Peter. He preached boldly and with Pentecostal power, and the multitude was smitten by the Holy Spirit. Yes, this is the self-same Simon Peter who denied his Lord — and cursed and lied in the process. Now Simon was bold and powerful because of the empowering of the Holy Spirit. Before this time he was outspoken and forceful in the strength of the flesh. Now he was in the anointing of the Spirit.

Can you imagine it? This was the same Simon — but not exactly. He was changed by the purging and purifying power of the Spirit.

Of the apostles, Peter was the most enthusiastic. At Caesarea Philippi, Jesus asked the apostles who people thought He was. John the Baptist? Elijah? Who? Peter, never to be outdone, answered rightly, "You are the Christ, the Son of the living God!"

And Jesus replied, "Blessed are you, Simon Bar-Jonah, for flesh and blood has not revealed this to you, but My Father who is in heaven. And I also say to you that you are Peter {*petros,* little stone, pebble} and on this rock {*petra,* big rock — actually Jesus Himself and the confession that He is the Christ} I will build My church, and the gates of Hades shall not prevail against it" (see Matt. 16:13–19). What an exchange!

And this was the man who would fight for Jesus until the end. He had boasted, "Lord, I'll never leave You. I'll stick with You." Yes, he had boasted of his faithfulness and tenacity. One time Peter thought Jesus was hinting at His own death, and blurted out) "Lord, let me go with you that I may also die." Ah, he talked a good game. He was rough and tough.

And do you recollect the time that Peter saw Jesus walking on the water? He thought to himself, *I'm going to step out on the waves myself.* He was so adult and yet so immature and childish! So, he jumped out of the boat and started walking to his Lord: (1) because he wanted to walk on the water, and (2) because he wanted to be with Him. He desperately wanted to be with Jesus. But, brave Simon Peter, the "rock," saw the commotion of the waves, became afraid, and sank like a rock indeed! It was a blessing that he didn't drown — if it hadn't been for Jesus, he probably would have.

Remember when the Roman soldiers and temple guards apprehended Jesus in the garden of Gethsemane? Peter pulled a sword from beneath his clothing and impetuously whacked off Malchus' servant's ear. Jesus calmly reached out and healed the man's ear.

And who can forget the early hours of the morning when Jesus was going through a mock trial and court? Peter and all the disciples except John had run for their lives. Even though he was guilt-ridden and haunted by his denial, Peter tried to follow Jesus from afar. He no doubt remembered Jesus' rebuke. And he heard Jesus' prophetic words, "Peter, before the rooster crows in the morning, you will betray me!" Yet, he wanted to be near Jesus. He reminds us of a pyromaniac who often wants to watch the destructive fire he has built.

How could Peter have that kind of nerve? Somehow the people in the courtyard recognized the stamp of Jesus on Simon. "There he is. He's one of those who follows the Galilean. Yes, he ought to be arrested!" Peter kept on denying it, but they yelled, "That's him, that's him. He's a disciple of the man from Galilee." And, to reinforce his lie, Peter resorted to cursing his Lord.

Peter, you traitor! You turncoat! You Benedict Arnold! But Peter went out and wept bitterly. His were tears of true repentance. Judas wept for different reasons.

After Jesus arose from the dead, one of His appearances was with Peter by the seaside. Jesus must have stung Peter by asking him three times to remind him of three denials, by saying, "Do you love Me?"

"Yes, Lord, you know that I love You," Peter said. Peter became the caretaker of the sheep, Jesus' sheep.

At Pentecost, Peter was turned inside out and transformed from a coward to a champion for Jesus Christ. Now he had been baptized, indwelt, sealed, was filled with the Holy Spirit, and anointed with power.

There will never be a church that is a great church in the eyes of God without a bold *proclamation* of the Word of God by a God-anointed and God-appointed preacher.

Gospel proclamation became the central part of the day. The preaching of the Gospel should be central in the church of the Lord Jesus Christ. It is still in this 21st century, by the "foolishness of preaching" that people are drawn to repentance. It is not simply enough to have the power of the gospel; great churches are also characterized by the proclamation of the gospel, GuideStone #2. We now turn our attention to Peter's pattern of Biblical exposition in the Pentecostal proclamation. To begin, it was:

# Prophetic proclamation

Our preaching must be prophetic. In other words, it must be biblical. Peter stood up before the crowd, raised his voice, opened the scroll to the prophet Joel, and read Joel 2:28–32. He established a scriptural basis for what was happening, and for what he desired his hearers to do in response. He then illustrated his text with Psalm 16 and Psalm 110. His preaching was prophetic and biblical. It is amazing how so many preachers do not seem to preach the Word of God today. A preacher who is not using the Bible would be like a surgeon going into surgery without his scalpel, because preaching the Word is what "cut to the heart" (Acts 2:37). For a preacher not to use the Word of God would be like a carpenter trying to build a home without a hammer. God spoke to us through Jeremiah saying, "Is not my word like a hammer that breaks a rock to pieces?" No wonder so many churches are empty. Our preaching must be prophetic.

Throughout church history the great, God-blessed churches in the world have had one common characteristic: an insistence upon an exposition of God's infallible Word. The men behind their pulpits selected their text from the Word of God and proclaimed it boldly. Peter chose a text from the prophet Joel. Joel had predicted that the Lord would come and visit His people. He prophesied that the

Lord would come and live in the midst of them, and that after this supernatural visitation He would "pour out his Spirit upon all flesh." Peter asserted, "this is what was spoken by the prophet Joel" (Acts 2:16). The text was happening before their eyes.

The Bible records, "Now when they heard this, they were cut to the heart" (Acts 2:37). What is it that cuts one's heart and pricks one's spirit? It is the sword, the Word of God.

The Word of God is profitable. Paul wrote to his young preacher-friend, Timothy, to remind him that "All Scripture is given by inspiration of God, and is profitable for doctrine, for reproof, for correction, for instruction in righteousness, that the man of God may be complete, thoroughly equipped for every good work" (2 Tim. 3:16–17). The Word of God is indeed profitable. It is profitable for four things: doctrine, reproof, correction, and instruction in righteousness. An effective ministry of God's Word will do all four. It will teach doctrine, rebuke and reprove sin, correct false paths, and train and instruct in righteousness.

There are churches today that have instructed in doctrine to the virtual exclusion of instructing in righteousness or correcting false paths. These groups are dying because of their emphasis on doctrine alone.

Other churches have emphasized reproof. They feel their God-given call is continuously to speak on how long someone's hair is or how short someone's dress is. They seldom, if ever, teach doctrine or instruct in righteousness.

There are still others who have pointed out correction to the virtual exclusion of doctrine, reproof, and instruction. Like those who have stressed reproof, they are polemic and think God has called them to correct everyone else while the lost world sits by watching and quietly going to hell.

Still others have emphasized instruction in righteousness of being Holy Spirit filled to the virtual exclusion of ever teaching doctrine. This constant emphasis on the deeper life without any strong doctrinal teaching, preaching, reproof, or correction has led to more than one division in the local body of believers.

An effective ministry of God's Word will be a balanced ministry and will do all four vital things. The Bible is profitable when it is used in a prophetic sense. As we look at Simon Peter's sermon, we find all four of these elements included. He taught doctrine as he spoke of the Deity of Christ (Acts 2:31–33, 36). He reproved sin (Acts 2:23). He corrected false paths and instructed in righteousness (Acts 2:38). Peter preached a balanced, biblical, prophetic message.

First, the proclamation of the gospel must be prophetic. The only way it can be prophetic is to be biblical. As we stop here at GuideStone #2, we see the importance of the prophetic proclamation of the gospel.

## Plain proclamation

Second, it must also be plain. In Acts 2:14, Peter proclaimed, "let this be known to you, and heed my words." The NIV puts it like this, "Let us explain this to you…" He was being *plain* in his approach. Peter did not make it difficult; he simply laid out the plain truth of the Word of God. He preached about sin, God's mercy in Christ, and the coming judgment, and the common people understood him. Many preachers today make their message difficult to understand. This gospel, of which we are stewards, is plain enough for a child to understand. Many churches never make an impact, because they do not preach the plain gospel. People can attend some churches for months (maybe even years) and never know what they must do to have eternal life.

The first Christian sermon was Christ-centered. Peter preached Christ. He preached about Jesus in His incarnation, death, resurrection, and presence by His Spirit. Peter did not preach systematic theology or philosophy, he preached Jesus: He was born to save, died on the cross, arose again, ascended, and is coming again. He did not preach theology. But he used theology to preach Christ. Peter was *plain* in his approach. He sent the message home:

"Him, being delivered by the determined purpose and foreknowledge of God, you have taken by lawless hands, have crucified, and put to death" (Acts 2:23).

Who crucified our Lord? The Jews? The Romans? No! I did, and you did — my sin, your sin. But in the truest sense — God did! No one took our Lord's life; He laid it down.

Peter was *plain* in the message of the gospel. The transparent truth is that the cross was no accident. Some people think the cross was some sort of a remedial action, kind of like a last-minute band-aid on a wounded world when everything else had failed. No! A thousand times, no!

It was the program and plan of God. Peter continued in Acts 2:23: "Him, being delivered by the determined purpose and foreknowledge of God, you have taken by lawless hands, have crucified, and put to death." The word translated *purpose* in the *New King James Version* of the Bible is the Greek word *boule.* It means God's irrevocable will, which will be done with or without our cooperation or consent.[1]

There is another word, translated in to our English words *counsel or purpose* which in Greek is *thelema,* simply meaning desire. We do not find that word in Acts 2:23. Instead, we discover the stronger word *boule.*

Therefore, what Peter was preaching to the crowd is this: There is nothing you could do that could have stopped or altered God's plan for the atonement of our sins at Calvary! God was in control. The Lord Jesus was handed over to you by God's "boule," God's irrevocable will, which was to be done with or without our cooperation or response.

Peter's message was plain. He preached Jesus. What makes a great church? It must have the element of proclamation, which is prophetic and plain.

## Positive proclamation

Third, proclamation must also be positive. Peter continued: "This Jesus God has raised up, of which we are all witnesses" (Acts 2:32). Peter unfurled the resurrection. The resurrection should be the heart of every sermon. Our Lord is not dead. He is alive! He is here and can meet our needs today. We have a *positive* gospel!

These disciples had seen the resurrected Christ, and He had transformed their lives. Most of them met martyrs' deaths. If they had been perpetrating a lie, they would not have died for their faith. Men do not die for a lie. Peter was crucified upside down in Rome. Being a martyr was one of the most marvelous proofs of the resurrection. Peter had seen the risen Lord. Jesus was alive! The resurrection should inject a positive note into our preaching, not some sort of superficial, pumped-up mental attitude. Every preacher should ask himself how much of his preaching points to the living Christ.

So many of our congregations today argue, "I've got to see it, and then I'll believe it."

But God says just the opposite, "You believe it, and then you'll see it."

Remember Thomas in the upper room? He struggled about this point, "I'll have to see it; then I'll believe it."

Jesus, appearing in His resurrected body, left this with him, "Thomas, blessed are those who have not seen and yet have believed." Where can we gain our positive spirit in preaching? We do not receive it from positive thinking or from possibility thinking. We should gather it from the same event Peter did, and that is the resurrection. The Lord Jesus is alive, and therefore our proclamation should be positive. There is not a need in the heart of any hearer that the living Christ cannot meet!

It was a hot, June day in Ada, Oklahoma. Early that morning I was pacing the second floor corridor at Valley View Hospital. It was a special day for our family, as our little Holly was making her grand entrance into our world. It was not long until Dr. Stevens appeared in the nursery windows and held that tiny package of love, wrapped in a pink blanket. He laid her in a bassinet and wheeled her over to the window where I could have a good look. Only a daddy can know the joy of that moment. I stood there alone for several minutes, thanking the Lord and watching that little red-faced beauty waving her arms, kicking her feet, and crying at the top of her lungs.

Suddenly, I noticed I was no longer standing there alone. A maid with her mop bucket was looking over my shoulder. "Is that your baby?" she asked. "Surely is," I proudly answered.

She continued, "Well, it's no wonder she's crying, being born into the world she has been born into." And then she turned around and sauntered down the hall, pushing her mop bucket before her.

For a moment I began to think, *She is right, If I believe everything I preach and teach, then it would be far better for this little girl to go on to heaven. After all, she would not have to go through all the heartaches of life and never have the haunting longing that some moment could be lived over.* I began to pray. It was an intimate moment with Jesus, Holly, and me. I often pray hymns in my private devotional time, and that morning the Holy Spirit began to pray, through me, the words of a Bill Gaither hymn, "Because He Lives." When I began the second verse of the hymn, I knew I was on holy ground:

"How sweet to hold a new born baby,
And feel the pride, and joy he gives;
But greater still the calm assurance,
This child can face uncertain days
…because he lives.
Because he lives I can face tomorrow;
Because he lives, all fear is gone;
Because I know he holds the future,
And life is worth the living just because he lives.[2]"

What makes a church great in the eyes of God? It is not only made up of the power of the gospel, but also the *proclamation of the gospel.* And our proclamation must be *prophetic, plain* and *positive.*

## Personal proclamation

Fourth, preaching must also be personal. Although Peter was preaching to a multitude of people, he was preaching on a personal level. Hear him as he says, "*Him,* being delivered by the determined purpose and fore-knowledge of God, *you* have taken by lawless hands, have crucified, and put to death" (Acts 2:23, author's italics). Note the personal pronouns. Preaching today is mostly in the first person plural or the third person plural. That is, we use a lot of "*we*" and "*they*" in our preaching. This type of preaching seldom brings about conviction. Peter preached in second person, saying, "Him, being delivered by the determined purpose and foreknowledge of God, you have taken by lawless hands, you have crucified, and you have put to death." You, you, you!

There are many preachers today who are afraid of offending deacons, elders, vestrymen, big givers, this person or that person, that civic leader or politician. It is no wonder many churches today have such little power. Our procla-mation should be personal. There is not much personal preaching today. Peter's preaching was not aimed just at the head but also at the heart. It was personal, and when he finished, the Bible reports, "Now when they heard this, they were cut to the heart" (Acts 2:37).

What makes a church great in the eyes of God? The element of proclamation is vital. Our preaching must not only be *prophetic*, *plain*, and *positive*, it must also be *personal*.

## Penetrating proclamation

Fifth, it must also be penetrating. Acts 2:37 tells us, "Now when they heard this, they were cut to the heart, and said to Peter and the rest of the apostles, 'Men and brethren, what shall we do?'" What happened? The Word testifies that the people's hearts were "cut." We have a word for that; we call it conviction. Much modern preaching is superficial, designed to meet "felt needs" in order to make the hearers feel good. I have heard preachers in some churches even boast that people can come to their services and never feel guilty about their lifestyles. They advertise that they are there to "make you feel good." Well, Peter's sermon "cut his hearers to the heart." The truth is, the only way we'll ever feel good about ourselves is to see ourselves for who we are, to confess that our sin put Christ on the cross and repent. Once we realize this and are set free through the blood of Jesus Christ, we will have the best feeling we've ever had.

Then we'll be able to sing:

"Free from the law, Oh happy condition
Jesus bled and there is remission
Cursed by the fall, condemned by the law
Christ has redeemed us, once for all."

*Lyrics by P. P. Bliss*

Until a person sees that there is no hope within himself to satisfy the righteous demands of the law, the cross is simply a farce to him. When conviction of sin arrives, we are aware that the only way we can get right with God is through the cross of our Lord Jesus Christ. Some people have never felt conviction. Their hearts have never been cut. Why? Because in too many cases they have not been under the preaching of the gospel which is prophetic, plain, positive, and personal. Few pulpits today urge men and women to take personal responsibility for their sin. No wonder, conversion is a lost word in our Christian vocabulary.

When these men and women at Pentecost realized what they had done in crucifying the Lord Jesus Christ, their hearts were broken. Why aren't more people's hearts cut in our churches today? It is because they do not realize that they ought to assume personal responsibility for their sin. And why? Because there is not enough preaching today which is penetrating. There are few preachers who even mention sin today. Many who advocate the New Trendy gospel pride themselves in never mentioning it. Sin is often the forgotten word in the pulpit today. No wonder many churches are dead and dying and others are so superficial even though they may have "crowds." There is no conviction in them, and without conviction there can be no conversion!

Conviction always precedes conversion. These people were "cut to the heart." This was a recognition of sin. Here is a broken and contrite heart. This process is called spiritual birth, and it is pictured in physical birth. There must be birth pains before the child is born, and so it is in spiritual birth. We cannot experience the new birth without godly sorrow over sin any more than one can give natural childbirth without experiencing birth pains. Conviction leads to conversion.[3] A host of people make some sort of "decision" early in life but have never really realized that they have personally sinned and put Christ on the cross. They were never really "cut to the heart" because of their sin.

Here, in Acts 2, we find the first account of the convicting work of the Holy Spirit. Jesus had prophesied the night before the crucifixion, "Nevertheless I tell you the truth. It is to your advantage that I go away; for if I do not go away, the Helper will not come to you; but if I depart, I will send Him to you. And when He has come, He will convict the world of sin, and of righteousness, and of judgment: of sin, because they do not believe in Me" (John 16:7–9).

While in my first pastorate at Hobart, Oklahoma, I learned a lot from those southwestern Oklahoma wheat farmers. In fact, I learned more from those dear, old men who had spent a lifetime in the Book of God than I did from a few of my professors. Being a city boy, I was fascinated by farm life. I learned there were several things necessary in order to grow a good crop.

First, the ground had to be broken. Farmers would use their tractors and plows and turn the sod over and over, breaking up the dirt. Second, the seed had to be planted. Third, the wheat was cultivated, watered, and nurtured.

Finally, about the first of June every year, the harvest was gathered!

Many churches today wonder why they never reap a harvest. Perhaps they have never broken ground! The Word of God cuts to the heart, and often there is not a great deal of preaching regarding the Word of God. Our preaching must be penetrating. We will never see the harvest if we do not preach the Word of God. It doesn't matter whether the seed is planted or whether the ground is cultivated, if it is not first broken, there will be no harvest.

What makes a church great? The power of the gospel and the proclamation of the gospel. Our proclamation should be *prophetic, plain, personal* and *penetrating.*

## Persuasive proclamation

Sixth, it must also be persuasive. Acts 2:37 says, "Now when they heard this, they were cut to the heart, and said to Peter and the rest of the apostles, 'Men and brethren, what shall we do?'" God-anointed preaching is *persuasive* preaching. It goes straight to the heart, and people begin to ask what was asked in this text, "What shall we do?" What a burning question! One who is convicted does not know what to do. It is not in the natural man's heart. It is "not by works of righteousness which we have done, but according to His mercy He saved us" (Titus 3:5, KJV).

Much preaching today falls on deaf ears, and often it is not the hearer's fault. At least many hearers are there, in their place and in their pew. Much of the preaching today is not persuasive, because in place of being plain it is complicated; in place of being positive it is critical; in place of being personal it is courteous, so as not to offend; and in place of being penetrating it is often cosmetic. No wonder modern preaching is not leading more people to ask, "What shall we do?"

What shall we do? This is the basic question we must ask in the the 21st century. What shall we do? It is not enough to be sorry for our sin. What shall we do? The question has a real ring of desperation in it. What shall we do? It is like the Philippian jailer who asked, "What must I do to be saved?" (Acts 16:30).

On the Day of Pentecost the hearers were "cut to the heart" (Acts 2:37). Note when they asked the question, "What shall we do?" It was when they heard Peter say in the previous verse, "Therefore let all the house of Israel know assuredly that God has made this Jesus, whom you crucified, both Lord and Christ." Jesus is Lord! He is risen from the dead, and He is Lord. This confronts us all with the question, "What shall we do?" What shall we do about the Lordship of Jesus Christ? Josh McDowell says He is either Lord or liar, and our eternal destiny hinges upon what we believe about this fact.

If the church in America today had sufficient power, today's masses, as the crowd did at Pentecost, would first be asking, "What does this mean?" (Acts 2:12). Then they would be asking, "What shall we do?" (Acts 2:37). Our preaching must be persuasive.

## Pointed proclamation

Seventh, our preaching must also be pointed. Peter answered their question with a pointed reply by saying, "repent" (Acts 2:38). He commanded his hearers as to what they ought to do. He did not give them several multiple-choice options. He was pointed. In a word he replied, "repent." What shall we do? Repent. Much preaching today is so vague. People can sit in some churches for months without any idea of how to apply the message to their lives on Monday through Friday. Preaching must not only be prophetic, it must be *pointed.*

Peter's pointed proclamation was in a word — *repent.* There are three pertinent questions to be asked at this point: *What is repentance? Why is repentance important? And where is repentance found in the salvation process?*

*First, what is repentance?* There seems to be considerable confusion regarding what repentance is. Let's look first at what repentance is *not.* Repentance is not *remorse.* It is not simply being sorry for our sin. Remorse may lead to repentance, but remorse is not repentance. The rich, young ruler went away very sorrowful when Jesus explained the demands of discipleship. He was remorseful, but he did not repent. Many people have substituted remorse for repentance.

Repentance is not *regret.* That is, it is not merely wishing some sinful deed, word, or action had not occurred. Pontius Pilate ceremonially took a basin of water and washed his hands, regretting his evil deed, but he did not repent. Many people substitute regret for repentance and tragically fool themselves in the process.

Repentance is not *resolve.* All of us have made New Year's resolutions. Many of us resolve to assume a new set of moral standards and live life on a higher plane but never seem able to turn that "new leaf over" for any considerable period of time. We cannot substitute resolve for repentance. It is not enough to sing "I Am Resolved," unless that is coupled with "godly sorrow," unless the repentance is genuine within one's heart, and unless there is a determination wrought by the Holy Spirit, in which one never wants to sin again, even though such is impossible as long as we are encased in the human flesh. But there must be that determination nonetheless. Genuine repentance is characterized by the person saying to himself and God, "I never want to displease the Lord again. I am so sorry for my sins. I am leaving that old life behind me. I don't want to be the same. I want to be changed by the Holy Spirit."

Through the years, I have heard more people make resolves that they have never followed. They bargained with the Lord, "0, Lord, if you just get me out of this mess, I'll do whatever You want. I'll follow wherever you lead. Lord, just help me." And the Lord does help them; they get out of their jam. And what happens? They go on living as they did before, making a mockery out of God, ignoring Him, and never looking back to those resolutions, because they were not accompanied by real repentance and doing a right about-face from sin. A mere resolution will not suffice.

Repentance is not *reform*. Sometimes reformation even involves restitution. It was so with Judas Iscariot. After betraying our Lord, he grabbed the 30 pieces of silver, returned to the temple and threw it at those who had paid the price of betrayal. Judas reformed, but unfortunately he did not repent. Many people today have substituted reform for repentance. Peter did not preach on the Day of Pentecost and say, "Reform." Nor did he say, "Resolve." Nor did he say, "Regret." Nor did he say, "Have remorse." His message was a pointed call for repentance.[4]

We have seen what repentance is not; now let us examine what repentance is. Is repentance turning from every sin as some people preach today? If so, then who has repented? When you came to Christ, did you turn from every sin you had ever committed? The truth is, in our natural state we are spiritually dead, not sick, and therefore unresponsive to the gospel. The Bible reminds us: "The natural man receiveth not the things of the Spirit of God: for they are foolishness to him: neither can he know them, because they are spiritually discerned" (1 Cor. 2:14, KJV). What is repentance? The word *repent* is the Greek word *metanoeo,* which in its original language is defined as a change of mind.[5] It is to change one's way of thinking about salvation. Repentance makes you love what you once hated, and hate what you once loved. When I was converted at age 17, I had never heard the word *repentance.* In fact, it was some weeks or perhaps months after my conversion before I ever remember hearing the word. But I know I repented! How do I know? The bad things I used to love, I no longer desired, and the things I never thought I would like became the things I loved to do. It was a change of mind. And God did it in me.

*Repentance is a change of mind.* Repentance involves a change of your mind about your own self, a change of your mind about sin, and a change of your mind about salvation. It is a change of mind that is always evidenced in three areas.

First, *attitude* is changed — that is, intellectually. As stated, it is a change of mind. This is where we begin. This is repentance.

Second, there is a change in the *affections* — the heart. If one genuinely changes one's mind, then a change of heart will follow.

The third result of a change of mind is a change in *action.* There will be a change in one's will or volition. If we genuinely changed our minds, our hearts will be changed, and if our hearts have been changed, a change in our will will follow. Paul said, "Therefore, if anyone is in Christ, he is a new creation; old things have passed away; behold, all things have become new" (2 Cor. 5:17). If we have experienced salvation our lives will be altered. We will no longer look at life, ourselves, and others as we once did. Like the prodigal son, God will give us new wishes and desires. This is repentance!

Since repentance is a change of mind, a person may be moved to tears emotionally by a sermon, and one's heart may overflow with remorse or regret, but it is not necessarily repentance. A person may have one's will manipulated by various means, but if he or she has not repented (changed one's mind), he or she is not saved. Jesus made it clear, "Except ye repent, ye shall all likewise perish" (Luke 13:3, KJV).

We find our most obvious biblical illustration of repentance in Luke 15 with the story of the prodigal son. Here was a young man who had gone to a far country and wasted all of his inheritance on ungodly living. He was far away from home. First of all, this boy came to have *a change of attitude.* Luke 15:17 (KJV) notes "he came to himself"— that is, he changed his mind. Then what happened? He had *a change of affection.* He thought to himself,

> "How many of my father's hired servants have bread enough and to spare, and I am perishing with hunger!
>
> I will arise and go to my father, and will say unto him, Father, I have sinned against heaven, and before thee,
>
> And am no longer worthy to be called thy son" (Luke 15:17–19, KJV).

His heart was changed. Then what happened after his change of mind resulted in a changed heart? He had *a change of action;* his will was changed, and so was his direction. "I will arise and go to my father." And Luke 15:20 states: "He got up and went to his father." The prodigal son had a change of mind. That was repentance. It was evident in four areas. He regretted his deed; he blamed himself for his sin; he acknowledged his father's right to be displeased, as he felt he was no longer worthy to be called his father's son; and he resolved to sin no more. After this, he went home. Repentance is a change of mind. The battle is in the mind, and the proof is in these four areas. Each of us will repent when we change our minds, and in changing our minds, our hearts will be changed. Therefore, a change in our will and volition will follow. This change of mind will cause us to regret our deed and blame ourselves for it, take responsibility for the deed, and resolve to set our face toward the Lord Jesus Christ.

By now it should be apparent why repentance is important. To begin with, it was the message of the Old Testament prophets, who were all preachers of repentance. As far back as Noah, we hear them calling on the people to forsake their wicked ways and turn to the Lord.

It was the message of the forerunner, John the Baptist: "Repent, for the kingdom of heaven is at hand!" (Matt. 3:2).

And Matthew 3:7–8 says, "But when he saw many of the Pharisees and Sadducees coming to his baptism, he said to them, 'Brood of vipers! Who warned you to flee from the wrath to come? Therefore bear fruits worthy of repentance.'"

Let's face it. I doubt if John the Baptist could make it as a pastor in most churches today. His preaching was pointed. He preached without fear or favor. He laid the ax to the tree. He didn't care who it offended, if God laid the message on his heart. He is the antithesis of much of the modern preaching that is heard today. He would not receive many invitations to preach in the New Trendy gospel church of today.

John the Baptist denounced Herod for adultery. He referred to his listeners as vipers and snakes. How long would a preacher last, if he called his listeners snakes, unless he were preaching to real snakes — the kind that slither and have forked tongues? And what kind of response did he receive? Well, the common people rejoiced over his straightforward ministry. However, the folks at the palace didn't like him. Herodias asked Herod for John's (decapitated) head on a platter in exchange for an exotic dance from Salome. John the Baptist was imprisoned and then beheaded for preaching the truth pointedly.

*It was the message of the Lord Jesus Himself.* He commenced His ministry with the message of repentance. The

Bible reports, "From that time Jesus began to preach and to say, 'Repent, for the kingdom of heaven is at hand.' " (Matt. 4:17). And in Mark 1:14–15: After John was put in prison, Jesus went into Galilee, proclaiming the good news of God. "The time has come," he said. "The kingdom of God is near. Repent and believe the good news!"

Jesus continued His ministry with the message of repentance by saying, "I tell you, no; but unless you repent you will all likewise perish" (Luke 13:3). The burden of His heart was in a word — *repent*. Jesus concluded His ministry with the word *repentance* as recorded in Luke 24:46–47, "This is what is written: The Christ will suffer and rise from the dead on the third day, and repentance and forgiveness of sins will be preached in his name in all nations."

One of the greatest books on evangelism that I have ever read is *With Christ After the Lost* by L. R. Scarborough, former president of Southwestern Baptist Theological Seminary. Let me share a few of his words with you:

*The Winning Characteristics of Jesus' Preaching*

1.  Its simplicity, utilizing everyday illustrations, simple but pungent words,
2.  Its positiveness and divine authority,
3.  Its heart-searching, bone-breaking, conviction-bringing power,

4. Its richness and abundance of fundamental doctrine and principles,
5. Its supreme tenderness and love, often mingled with scathing, blistering denunciation,
6. Its direct and personal reach,
7. Its unfailing appeal to the highest in man and God.[6]

Jesus' first sermon was "Repent and believe the good news." It was also the message of the Great Commission. In Matthew's account of this, God gives us the mechanics. We are to *make* disciples, *mark* disciples by baptism, and *mature* disciples by teaching them to observe the faith. These are the *mechanics* of the Great Commission.

Mark's account gives us the *measure* of it. We are commanded to take the gospel to the whole world.

In Luke's account of the Commission, he gave us the message of the Great Commission. What is it? "That repentance and remission of sins should be preached…among all nations" (Luke 24:47, KJV). Jesus *commenced, continued,* and *concluded* His ministry with the same word — repent. How can a minister today claim to be preaching the gospel of Jesus Christ if he leaves out the heart of our Lord's message? *Our preaching must be pointed.*

Repentance was also the message of the apostles. "So they went out and preached that people should repent"

(Mark 6:12). They went out and preached. What did they preach? Prosperity? Successful living? Felt needs? No, they went out and preached that people should repent.

It was the message of Simon Peter. Hear him at Pentecost, raising his voice in his mighty sermon, and answering the question of what the people should do with a one-word reply — "Repent!"

Scarborough summed up the characteristics of Simon Peter:

> "But Peter's greatest distinction is that he was the Evangelist of Pentecost. His voice and ministry introduced the age and ministry of the Holy Ghost. John the Baptist introduced Jesus, and Peter introduced the Holy Spirit to a lost world. He preached the first sermon in the world under the vice-regency of the Divine Spirit after Christ's ascension."[7]

Scarborough continued concerning Peter:

> "1. His simple straightforwardness of character and manner...He had no dignity to bother him. He was hampered by no sacred traditions. He struck straight. Dignities, ministerial stiffness, conventionalities and all such hinder; Gospel evangelism and the true approach to souls. Peter went after lost

men like he sought the finny tribe of stormy Galilee — cast his net in where the fish were and pulled them into his boat.

2. He preached plain, unvarnished truth right out without apology or compromise. He saw men as sinners and realized — their need was Christ and knew that the Gospel revealed Christ to them. He threw a hot Gospel at the bared souls of men in great golden chunks. His sermon on the Day of Pentecost is packed with doctrine…He did not mince matters. He dodged nothing."[8]

Repentance was also the message of the apostle Paul. Hear him: "Truly, these times of ignorance God overlooked, but now commands all men everywhere to repent" (Acts 17:30). Hear him later: "testifying to Jews, and also to Greeks, repentance toward God and faith toward our Lord Jesus Christ" (Acts 20:21).

It was also the message of John the beloved apostle. Simply turn to the message directed to the churches of Asia, as recorded in the early chapters of Revelation, and discover that eight times, in letters to the seven churches, he pealed forth the message of repentance. Why is it important? Because it is the message of the Bible.

What was the message of the Bible? What was the message of the early church? Was it positive thinking, with all sorts of trinkets for reminders? Was it concentrated ministries on the home, ministries on finance, or selected other "professional ministries"? Was it a "felt needs" approach? When we read the Book of Acts, we find none of these in the early church. Why? Their message was "repent."

This is what accounts for a happy home — when a husband and wife repent. We can fill out workbooks until we are blue in the face and sit before videotaped seminars until we can sit no longer (and many of those are good), but I believe what the church severely needs today is the message of repentance. When a person genuinely repents, he or she will put one's home in order.

It is strange how many preachers are silent today concerning the message of repentance, especially when it is the theme of the message of not only the Old Testament preachers, not only the apostles, but of the Lord Himself. It could be that some have lost sight of the sinfulness of mankind. Today some are preaching who deny the Bible truth of a literal, burning hell, or at least they never mention it. There are many preachers today who hold the doctrine of inclusivism, believing that ultimately and eventually everyone will be saved. Consequently, what need is there for the message of repentance in these churches? Too many churches and preachers have lost sight of the lostness of humankind and the holiness of God. Perhaps it is because repentance is not a popular message. Of course, it is indeed more popular to "tickle the ears" of our listeners with messages of positive or possibility thinking.

This presents another question: Where is repentance in salvation? What did Peter mean in this Pentecostal sermon? Does repentance precede faith? Or does faith precede repentance? Think about it. Does one repent before one can exercise faith? If you believe repentance is turning from every sin, then faith must come first, because repentance would then become a work of salvation. This is the idea of some today.

But if repentance is turning from every sin, then who has repented? Conversely, if you believe that repentance is indeed a change of mind, then repentance is first in the order, because a person must change one's way of thinking before he or she can grasp the free promise, the grace of God in Christ Jesus. Now, since humankind is totally depraved and since God sovereignly calls us unto Himself, it stands to reason that God, then, must grant repentance to us, because we cannot obtain it in our own depraved condition.

This is exactly what the Bible teaches. Take for example 2 Timothy 2:24–25:

"And a servant of the Lord must not quarrel but be gentle to all, able to teach, patient, in

humility correcting those who are in opposition,
if God perhaps will grant them repentance, so that
they may know the truth."

Repentance is the gift of God's grace that transforms the mind. God grants unto us repentance. When the attitude is genuinely transformed, the heart is transformed, and this effects a change of action. Faith and repentance are as much the gifts of God as the Savior upon whom our faith rests. Salvation is from first to last, all of grace. Listen to Acts 5:31: "Him God has exalted to His right hand to be Prince and Savior, to *give repentance* to Israel and forgiveness of sins." (author's italics). The truth is our Lord Jesus has gone up so that grace might come down. Repentance is the gift of God given to us by Christ.

There is a positive motive that produces repentance. It is not so much the message of "bumper-sticker evangelism" which might read, "turn or burn." It is more the message found in the Roman letter where Paul says, "God's kindness [goodness] leads you toward repentance" (Rom. 2:4).

We are so privileged to hear the gospel: The gospel which billions of people on our planet have never heard. We are privileged to hear the message of repentance. Today, missionaries' feet have never before walked in so many little villages. A copy of God's Word has not been translated into the dialects and languages of some, and they die in the darkness; millions going down. And us? We are placed in the very spotlight of the Christian life. And yet, few of us have any time for the Lord Jesus. Can't we understand that it is the goodness of God which allows us to hear the gospel and that this is what leads us to repentance? Peter stood up and shouted, "Repent!"

The Bible does not indicate that it is the kindness of God that *calls* us to repentance, but it says, "the kindness of God *leads* us to repentance." The truth is God calls us to repentance by the gospel, but God leads us to repentance by His goodness. The goodness of God comes to us where we are; takes us by the hand, as though we were a little child; and leads us to repentance. Yes, it is the goodness of God that leads us to repentance.

His amazing grace is offered freely through His goodness and mercy. He guides and leads the unconverted person to repentance toward God and faith in our Lord Jesus Christ (Acts 21:20). Many are the questions which frail humans raise. Doubters and others who have grown bitter remind me of an illustration I heard years ago. You see, the goodness, kindness, and love of God are like the sun. We could compare the heart to butter or mud. When the sun beats down on the butter, it melts. When the sun shines on the mud, it turns hard like brick. This is the nature of the human heart.

When the convicting Son of God shines upon some hearts, they melt like butter. When He beams upon other hearts, they turn to hardened brick. Only the goodness of God can lead us to repentance, and men and women must let Him do His work of repentance.

My family and I used to spend vacations in a quaint little village in the Great Smoky Mountains known as Maggie Valley. It is a refreshing retreat, far from the massive traffic jams and bustle of big city life. It is like stepping into a time tunnel; there are sights and sounds that we never see and hear in our metropolis.

One summer, when our girls were small, we rented an old, white farmhouse on the side of a mountain. It was a lovely spot, but a little scary for our two small, city girls. The children slept upstairs, and the whole house creaked whenever anyone took a step. The first night happened to be one of those pitch-black summer nights in the mountains. As James Weldon Johnson described in *God's Trombones,* "It was blacker than a hundred midnights down in a cypress swamp."

I was awakened in the middle of the night by the cries of our youngest daughter, who was only six or seven years old at the time. I bounded up the stairs to find her standing in the dark, calling for me. Taking her by the hand, I led her down the steps into the security of our bed where she slept soundly for the rest of the night. And so, our dear Heavenly Father finds us in the dark and takes us by the hand. The Bible gives a comforting word, "He leads us to repentance." When these men and women at Pentecost asked, "What shall we do?" Peter's reply came quickly. "Repent!" What should we do in our 21st century world? The Bible answers us plainly and clearly. Repent! Change our minds. Turn around. Go in a different direction.

So what is the message the church should be preaching today? Repentance. Peter was preaching: "You have missed God's offer of salvation. You are missing the purpose for which you were created."

What can you do about it? Change your mind![9] Change your mind about your sin. Change your mind about the Lord Jesus Christ. Change your mind about yourself. Change your mind about the plan of salvation. Note Peter's promise is that they would receive forgiveness. He did not promise them wind, fire, or tongues. The important aspect here is forgiveness of sin.

Note the conclusion of Acts 2:38: "Repent, and let every one of you be baptized in the name of Jesus Christ for the remission of sins; and you shall receive the gift of the Holy Spirit." Repent and what? Repent and be baptized! There is tremendous confusion and controversy over this verse today — in fact, for centuries this has been the case. Does this mean we must be baptized in order to have our sins removed? Some answer with an emphatic yes. It certainly appears so by this verse. But what does the Bible really mean here?

The key is found in the preposition, translated into our English word, *for*. It is the Greek word *eis*. This same Greek word is translated two ways in the English Bible. In some verses it is translated "*for*" or "*in order to*", and in other verses as "*because of*."[10] Now the same word is used in both instances. The meaning in Acts 2:38 is not *in order to* but *because of*. Think for a moment. Just with our English vernacular, we say, "He was electrocuted *for murder*." Does that mean *in order to* or *because of*? Or take for example the statement, "He has been rewarded for good grades."[11] Do we mean *in order to* or *because of*? Listen again to Acts 2:38: "Repent, and let every one of you be baptized in the name of Jesus Christ for the remission of sins; and you shall receive the gift of the Holy Spirit." What do you think it means? Be baptized in order to have your sins forgiven or be baptized because your sins are forgiven?

It becomes even more plain when we look into the Greek New Testament. For example, look at Matthew 12:41, where the same Greek word *eis* is translated *at*. "The men of Nineveh will rise up in the judgment with this generation and condemn it, because they repented at the preaching of Jonah; and indeed a greater than Jonah is here." The word *at* here is the Greek word *eis*. It is the same Greek word we find in Acts 2:38. The Ninevites repented *because of* the preaching of Jonah. I believe that the proper translation of the word *eis* is *because of*. Acts 2:38 can well and properly be translated, "Repent and be baptized *because of* the forgiveness of your sins." We should be baptized because our sins are forgiven, and it is an outward expression of the inward experience. We *are not* baptized because water will wash away a single sin and merit salvation for us.

Some claim that the phrase in Acts 2:38, "Be baptized, every one of you, in the name of Jesus Christ," is parenthetical. Those who adhere to this view do so from a grammatical viewpoint in the Greek. For example, the verb *repent* is plural and so is the pronoun *your*.[12] The imperative "be baptized" is singular. It is set off from the rest of the sentence in a parenthetical sort of way. Therefore, read the verse like this: "Repent for the forgiveness of your sins." This certainly fits with what the same preacher, Simon Peter, emphasized later in Acts 10:43: "To Him all the prophets witness that, through His name, whoever believes in Him will receive remission of sins." This same expression, "sins may be forgiven" is found in its use here at Caesarea. There is no mention here at Cornelius's house of baptism for salvation, although they were all baptized as a confession of their faith because their sins had been forgiven.

Whatever Peter meant in Acts 2:38, it must be understood that nowhere do the Scriptures teach that salvation is dependent upon water baptism. Twice in the Corinthian letter Paul states clearly what the gospel is, and baptism is certainly not included.

In 1 Corinthians 1:17, he wrote, "For Christ did not send me to baptize, but to preach the gospel, not with wisdom of words, lest the cross of Christ should be made of no effect." In I Corinthians 15:1–4, he penned these lines,

> "Moreover, brethren, I declare to you the gospel which I preached to you, which also you received and in which you stand, by which also you are saved, if you hold fast that word which I preached to you — unless you believed in vain.

> For I delivered to you first of all that which I also received: that Christ died for our sins according to the Scriptures, and that He was buried, and that He rose again the third day according to the Scriptures."

God-anointed preaching produces *conviction*. This leads to *conversion* and then to *confession*. This is the order. It begins with conviction (Acts 2:37), which leads to conversion and results in confession (Acts 2:38). Baptism is vitally important, not for conversion but for confession. It signifies outwardly what has occurred inwardly. Our preaching must be pointed. It must tell people what the text says and what it wants them to do. The Christian's primary desire should always be to win people to repentance toward God and faith in the Lord Jesus Christ. And what makes a great church in the eyes of God? There has never been a great church in the eyes of God that didn't make much of the preaching of the gospel that was prophetic, plain, positive, personal, penetrating, persuasive, and pointed.

## Pious proclamation

Eighth, preaching must also be pious. By pious we mean "God fearing." We are not talking about pious in the sense of its modern connotation, but pious in the sense that we fear God and realize that He is the sovereign Lord. That is what Peter meant when he used the phrase "as many as the Lord our God will call" (Acts 2:39). Our proclamation must be pious. Great preachers and teachers realize that God is sovereign and that He is the one who adds to the church; thus they have a real sense of dependence upon Him and a deeper desire to be faithful to His Word in life and lip.

Acts 2:39 is a key to understanding this vital principle. "For the promise is to you and to your children, and to all who are afar off, as many as the Lord our God will call." The promise is for all whom our Lord God will call. There are two types of calls — the outward call and the inward call.

Peter gave the outward call, but do you know who was saved that day? Not everyone there was saved. In fact, the Bible tells us that some of them mocked him. The ones who were saved that day were "all whom the Lord God called." Our proclamation must be pious in that we realize our job is faithfulness to the outward call and trust in the Lord Jesus by His Spirit to issue the inward call.

Through the years many people who have rejected the Lord have alibied to me, "Well, preacher, I just don't want to become a Christian now, but I will later, when I feel like the time is right." I have pointed out that you can't come to Jesus at your convenience. It has to be in *His time.* It must be when He calls.

This is why evangelists like Billy Graham have preached, in essence, so many times, "If you have the slightest impulse to come to Jesus Christ, do it now, because God has put that call into your heart. It may not come tomorrow."

"Now is the accepted time; behold, now is the day of salvation" (2 Cor. 6:2, KJV). That means the day of salvation is when God gives that inward call. For you to be truly saved, the Holy Spirit must be dealing with your heart. You must be under conviction.

In many churches today, the conviction of the Holy Spirit is never preached. Where there *is* no conviction, there can be no conversion. The apostle John in his Gospel quoted Jesus Himself as He prepared the apostles for His crucifixion, resurrection, and His ascension.

"I will not leave you comfortless: I will come to you" (14:18, KJV).

"And when he [Holy Spirit] is come, he will reprove the world of sin, and of righteousness, and of judgment:

Of sin, because they believe not on me,

Of righteousness, because I go to my Father, and ye see me no more;

Of judgment, because the prince of this world is judged" (16:8–11, KJV).

Who does the convicting? The Holy Spirit. Who does the convincing and converting? The Holy Spirit. And without convicting power working in one's life, you can never be saved.

As you read the lines, and you sense that you are unsaved, hope with all of your heart as you fall under conviction, that you will see your sins that have sent Jesus to the cross, and that you will see yourself as God presently sees you — undone, condemned, lost, but also as precious in His sight. Long for the conviction that will lead to your repentance and faith.

Consider the following words of our Lord at this very point:

"All that the Father gives Me will come to Me, and the one who comes to Me I will by no means cast out" (John 6:37).

"No one can come to Me unless the Father who sent Me draws him; and I will raise him up at the last day" (John 6:44).

Do you remember Jesus' declaration to Simon Peter after Peter's great confession at Caesarea Philippi? "Blessed are you, Simon Bar-Jonah, for flesh and blood has not revealed this to you, but My Father who is in heaven" (Matt. 16:17). Paul put it like this:

"For as many as are led by the Spirit of God, these are sons of God" (Rom. 8:14).

"But when it pleased God, who separated me from my mother's womb and called me through His grace" (Gal. 1:15).

Peter declared,

"But you are a chosen generation, a royal priesthood, a holy nation, His own special people, that you may proclaim the praises of Him who called you out of darkness into His marvelous light" (I Pet. 2:9).

"But may the God of all grace, who called us to His eternal glory by Christ Jesus, after you have suffered a while, perfect, establish, strengthen, and settle you" (I Pet. 5:10).

How can two people sit on the same pew in the same worship service, sing the same songs, hear the same sermon with the same anointing, and one of them feel absolutely no need of coming to Christ — or anything spiritual for that matter — and the other fall under deep conviction of sin and a longing to know Jesus personally? How can this happen? It happens by the inward call of God.

The most obvious Scripture illustration of this point is found in Acts 16, when Paul was preaching at the riverside near Philippi. The Bible records,

"Now a certain woman named Lydia heard us. She was a seller of purple from the city of Thyatira, who worshiped God. *The Lord opened her heart* to heed the things spoken by Paul" (Acts 16:14, author's italics).

Paul issued the outward call, and the Lord spoke to Lydia's heart, issuing the inward call.

There are a few extremists today who have carried these doctrines of grace to the point of perverting the Scripture by denying the free offer of the gospel, and in so doing have set their camps dangerously close to the border of heresy. The fact that salvation is God's work, and He takes the initiative in calling us, does not diminish one's intensity in preaching the gospel to every creature and sharing the outward call to every last person on this planet. We have a Great Commission to "preach the gospel to every creature" (Mark 16:15, KJV). This is why doctrines of grace should intensify our evangelistic efforts. We are to proclaim to the world the outward call and then trust the Holy Spirit to issue the inward call. Here again is this element of the participation of God in the call of the gospel.

To the person who literally believes in the Great Commission, it is inconceivable that any Christian could make rationalizations like these:

- God's going to save people when He pleases, without any help of mine or yours.

- I can't go because God's not ready for me yet.

- If God's going to save the heathen, He'll do it Himself without our interference.

We cannot comprehend it, but God has chosen frail, faulted people like you and me to be His messengers. Jesus declared in John 20:21: "As my Father hath sent *me*, even so send I you" (KJV). And what was Jesus sent to do? "For the Son of man is come to seek and to save that which was lost" (Luke 19:10, KJV). We cannot save them, but we are to seek them. God has called on us to extend the outward call. He does the inward work. We do the outward call under the leadership of the Holy Spirit.

The last invitation of the Bible says,

"And the Spirit and the bride say, 'Come!' And let him who hears say, 'Come!' And let him who thirsts come. Whoever desires, let him take the water of life freely" (Rev. 22:17).

Here we see the outward call and the inward call. The bride (the church of Jesus Christ) says come — this is the outward call. But there is also the inward call — the Spirit says come. What makes a great church? It must be a church that proclaims the Word of God in a sense that is totally dependent upon the Holy Spirit.

"Rescue the perishing,

Care for the dying,

Snatch them in pity

from sin and the grave;

Weep o'er the erring one,

Lift up the fallen,

Tell them of Jesus

the mighty to save.

Rescue the perishing, Care for the dying;

Jesus is merciful, Jesus will save."

*Lyrics by Fannie J. Crosby*[13]

# Persistent proclamation

Ninth, our proclamation of the gospel must also be persistent. The Bible says, "With *many* other words…he pleaded with them" (Acts 2:40). The English word translated *pleading* or *exhorting* is the word *parakeleo*. It means to beseech with strong force, to call forth. It is a calling to one side. Peter didn't preach, sit down, cross his legs, and look humble. He didn't preach and say, "Now let's sing a hymn, and if by chance anyone might possibly want to step forward for Christ, you can do so at this time, but please don't feel like you have to." Peter did not apologize. What did he do? He gave a gospel invitation. When he finished with his sermon, he pleaded for souls. "With many other words he pleaded with them."

My pastoral predecessor in Dallas, Dr. W. A. Criswell, the God-anointed pastor of First Baptist Church, Dallas, for 50 years advised us well. "As a famous London pastor lay dying, his friends gathered around and asked, 'Do you have one last word for the world?' The loving pastor replied: 'Yes, I do. Tell the pastors of the world this, Oh preacher, make it plain how a man can be saved!' "

When the pastor has shown the sinner that he is lost, when he has presented Christ's redemptive plan of salvation, then he is to draw the penitent into an open confession of his faith in Jesus (Matt. 10:32–33; Rom. 10:9–10).

How does he do that effectively? How can the pastor extend an invitation that pulls at the heartstrings of a lost man? Here are some suggestions to consider:

1.  It must be in the heart of the preacher to make an appeal to people. He must pray to this end that God will help him do it effectively...

2.  The sermon must lead up to this climactic consummation. Whatever the subject, the message must be turned to the soul for the grace and mercy of God...

3.  Many pastors close their sermons with a prayer while the heads of the people are bowed in prayer with him. In this prayer this pastor prays for the lost and for others who are to be included in the invitation...

4.  At the end of the prayer the congregation can be asked to stand as the choir begins to sing the invitation hymn...

5.  The invitation can be for anything the Spirit lays upon the heart of the pastor. Besides the appeal for the lost to confess their faith in the Lord, the invitation can be for baptism and church membership, the transfer of church letters, those who cannot get church letters to come forward by statement...

6.  Music plays an all-important part in this appeal..."[14]

There should always be an appeal *after* the gospel is preached. The reverse is also true. The gospel should always be preached *before* an appeal is given. We should never issue an appeal until after the gospel is preached.

Many of us have heard evangelists who tell one deathbed story after another, moving on the emotions of the hearers, never having within their message the "kerygma"— the fact that He who knew no sin became sin for us that we might become the righteousness of God in Him. There is considerable fallout of "new converts" due to this. Peter preached the gospel and then made an appeal; such is biblical and right. He pleaded for souls that day. He exhorted them. "With many words" he besought them with strong force to receive Christ.

He pleaded with them to "save yourselves from this corrupt generation." Although God takes the initiative, God *chooses, calls, convicts,* and *converts, we* must *confess.* We must identify with the Lord Jesus Christ. Paul said it this way, "For with the heart man believeth unto righteousness; and with the mouth confession is made unto salvation" (Rom. 10:10, KJV). Peter was calling for a decision. "With many other words he warned them; and he pleaded with them, 'Save yourselves from this corrupt generation'" (Acts 2:40).

For the true preacher of the gospel, preaching is not a profession; it is an obsession. In a sense, that is true for every believer. Every waking minute it is a part of our lives. Our proclamation must be *persistent.* There is a note of urgency here. What makes a church great in the eyes of God? The power of the gospel but also the proclamation of the gospel. Our preaching must be *prophetic, plain, positive, penetrating, persuasive, pointed, pious* and *persistent.*

## Productive proclamation

Tenth, it must also be productive. Acts 2:41 reported, "Then those who gladly received his word were baptized; and that day about three thousand souls were added to them." Three thousand precious persons were saved that day and followed the Lord in believer's baptism. It is apparent that the Bible doesn't speak a word about these newly baptized believers speaking in *glossa.* Although Acts 2:38 shows, "you will receive the gift of the Holy Spirit."

No doubt most of those converts at Pentecost were Jews. So far as we know, the first church was largely made up of Jews. It is wrong to think that all the Jews in the first century rejected the Christian religion. No! They were the first ones who really accepted Him. They accepted all that the prophets had foretold about the Messiah, and many saw Him as Jesus of Nazareth.

The truth about the Christian church is we don't ask Jewish people to convert to our religion; we have converted to theirs. The Lord Jesus is indeed the Jewish Messiah. Had you visited the first church in Jerusalem, you would have found it comprised almost totally of Jewish believers.

Some today insist that Jews have a special way of being saved apart from the Lord Jesus Christ. But Peter preached to them, "repent" (Acts 2:38). He called on them to change their minds about themselves, the Savior, their sin, and salvation. To whom was he speaking? Jews! Religious Jews. He was not afraid he would offend them. There are preachers today who will not even pray in the name of Jesus if Jewish people are present for fear of offending them. Listen to Peter as he answered their question of what they should do with the word "repent!"

Three thousand people were saved in one day! They did so much with so little, and we seem to do so little with so much! What a glorious picture here of Christ receiving sinners. He casts out none who trust in Him.

What makes a church great? The power of the gospel which involves unity and unction is vitally important. There has never been a great church in the eyes of God that didn't make much of Bible *proclamation* which was *prophetic, plain, positive, personal, penetrating, persuasive, pointed, pious, persistent* and *productive.*

Immersed in a world of modern church growth principles that often de-emphasize the importance of the proclamation of the gospel by means of expository preaching, it would do us well to remember that all roads lead back to Jerusalem. And along that road we have now come to GuideStone #2 which points us in the direction of expository preaching and warns us of a superficial discipleship that is not centered in the Word of God.

While writing this chapter, my morning devotional reading took me to the sixth chapter of Revelation. John's probing question should haunt every preacher of the gospel —"for the great day of His wrath has come, and who is able to stand?" (Rev. 6:17). What an awesome responsibility rests upon those who are called to preach the gospel. In the future when God's wrath is indeed poured out, will what we have been about endure or will it be consumed like "wood, hay and stubble?" What kind of a gospel did we preach? Was it penetrating? Did it cut the hearts of our hearers and bring genuine conviction of sin? Was it pointed? Did we call men and women to genuine repentance or is that one of the forgotten words in our preaching vocabulary? As John put it, "Who can stand?"

These early church leaders left us some important guidestones as reminders for our own journey. Here at GuideStone #2 we learn the importance of a pulpit ministry that issues out of God's Word which is always "profitable" and which "never returns void."

GuideStone #3

# The preservation
# of the gospel

*(Acts 2:41–46)*

A long the road on our journey back to Jerusalem we now come to GuideStone #3. It has been left for us by our spiritual forefathers to point the direction of the preservation of the gospel message and to warn of danger for the church if we do not pass along the "apostles' doctrine" to the next generation. Tragically, the call of much of modern church growth has with it a de-emphasis on the great doctrinal truths of the faith which have framed our beliefs for centuries. One of the signature marks of this early church was that they did not just start well but they "continued steadfastly in the apostles' doctrine" (Acts 2:42). They preserved doctrinal truth in their lifetime and faithfully passed it on to future generations. How did they accomplish this?

By continuing to teach doctrine and realizing they were what Paul would later call "stewards of the gospel."

The call to the exclusivity of the gospel is not a message that has "made in America" stamped upon it. It is good news that has "made in heaven" stamped on it, it was delivered to a Palestinian world 2,000 years ago in the body of Christ who "became flesh and dwelt among us", it was delivered to us through the faithfulness of the apostolic preachers and millions of martyrs through the centuries who gave their lives for this exclusive truth, and now, we are "stewards" of this gospel. Ours is an awesome responsibility. The Christian ministry to which we are called is a sacred stewardship. It is up to us to preserve this gospel message for the next generations. Paul saw himself as "God's steward" (Titus 1:7) and referred to himself and Apollos as "stewards of the mysteries of God" (1 Cor. 4:1). In the same Corinthian passage he went so far as to say that it is "required of stewards to be faithful." As we come to this third guidestone along the way to rediscovering the emphasis of church growth found in Jerusalem, we come face to face with the fact that it is not just our responsibility to live in the power of the gospel, nor simply to proclaim the gospel, but it is ours to preserve the gospel and, as we see in Jerusalem, to preserve the new converts with whom the Lord entrusts us.

As the early church began to grow we discover in Acts that their purpose for gathering together was primarily for the exaltation of Christ and the edification of the believers. It seems that in many of the New Trendy gospel churches the sole purpose of gathering is to create an atmosphere conducive and acceptable to the "seeker." This is in stark contrast to the approach of the New Testament church. They did not see their job as creating an atmosphere to get "seekers" into their church, but to so create an atmosphere where God could get in! The modern approach has inverted the great commission's call to "go and tell" and replaced it with "come and hear."

Acts 2:41–46 outlines for us the New Testament method for preserving the gospel and the converts with whom we are entrusted. It points us to three important areas — baptism, the Bible and the body-life concept. The scripture records:

> "Then those who gladly received his word were baptized; and that day about three thousand souls were added to them. And they continued stead-fastly in the apostles' doctrine and fellowship, in the breaking of bread, and in prayers. Then fear came upon every soul, and many wonders and signs were done through the apostles. Now all who believed were together, and had all things in common, and sold their possessions and goods,

and divided them among all, as anyone had need.

So continuing daily with one accord in the temple, and breaking bread from house to house, they ate their food with gladness and simplicity of heart" (Acts 2:41–46).

God-blessed churches are not only made up of those who appreciate the *power* of the gospel and *proclamation* of the gospel but also the *preservation* of the gospel. The Bible says these early believers "continued steadfastly in the apostles' doctrine and fellowship" (Acts 2:42, KJV). There are three elements involved in the *preservation* of new converts in the church of Jesus Christ. They are *baptism,* the *Bible* and *body life.*

One can never grow to Christian maturity apart from the Bible. Perhaps the worst problem in many churches is a host of spiritual infants who have never grown in their faith because they have been fed a diet of pop psychology and seeker sociology instead of New Testament theology.

A number of years ago two eight-year-old boys were brought to Orlando to the world-famous amusement parks. They each had a disease which aged their bodies far in advance of their years. While the boys were only children, their appearance was that of 80-year-old men. They were children who had grown old and were about to die but had never grown up.

As I watched those two boys on the newscast, I thought about how so many are like that in the church today. They are children who have grown old in the faith but have never grown up in some ways. This is a tragedy of the New Trendy gospel.

If you have ever had a baby in your home, there are some things you have readily observed. As much as you love them, babies do want their own way. They want what they want, when they want it! Also, you will note that babies seem basically lazy. That is, they lie around a lot. They don't (and can't) wash any of the dishes, make any of the beds, or pick up any of the dirty clothes. The fact is they've simply not grown enough to make "mature" decisions and perform certain duties.

Another obvious characteristic of a baby is that he or she is taken up with personalities. As far as we know, a baby can't look beyond a personality to have a spirit of discernment. The biggest mass murderer in America could come into their room and utter a few ga-ga's and goo-goo's and have a baby smiling. Another of the most evident characteristics of a baby is that he can play while big things are happening. Some families can be going through the heartache of divorce or death, while all the time the baby is down on the floor playing with a ball. Finally, babies get easily upset. If you don't believe it, just don't give a baby a bottle at the time she thinks she needs it and see her reaction!

All of the above are signs of babes in Christ. They may be 70 years old, but if they have never matured in their faith, their feelings are the same spiritually as those babies are physically. Babies in the church always want their own way. They have no spirit of submission. They are not interested in what other church members think. Babies in the church are basically lazy. You will not find them out on outreach night or involved in other ministries.

Like physical babies, they do not give of themselves in the realm of time, talent, or tithe. Also, they are unconcerned about others. They are taken up with personalities. They want to be entertained. They have no spirit of discernment between the spirit of good and the spirit of wrong. One of the most tragic facts about babies in the church is that, like physical babies, they play when big things are happening. Tremendous transformations take place in people's lives, and people are saved and pass from darkness into light, but it really makes no difference to a spiritual baby since his greatest concern is getting to the cafeteria line and making sure the service does not go past noon. Spiritual babies also become upset easily.

We know what children need. All they need is to grow up! And it is impossible to grow up as a Christian apart from the Word of God. The early church preserved their new converts and the way they did it was through baptism, the Bible, and body life.

# Believer's baptism

The first important element in preservation is believer's baptism. In Acts 2:38–41, Peter called upon his hearers to "repent and be baptized." Why? Because it is essential in preservation. As soon as these early believers were saved, they were immediately baptized. This is seen throughout the Book of Acts.

Today, we often hear some people talk about the fact that a new convert has to "prove" himself before being baptized, but this was certainly not the case in the early church.

Acts 8 recorded the baptism of the Ethiopian eunuch:

"Then Philip began with that very passage of Scripture and told him the good news about Jesus.

As they traveled along the road, they *came* to *some* water and the eunuch said, 'See, here is water. What hinders me from being baptized?'"

"Then Philip said, 'If you believe with all your heart, you may.'"

"And he answered and said, 'I believe that Jesus Christ is the Son of God.'"

"So he commanded the chariot to stand still. And both Philip and the eunuch went down into the water, and he baptized him" (vv. 36–38).

In Acts 10, there was baptism of the family of Cornelius:

"Can anyone forbid water, that these should not be baptized who have received the Holy Spirit just as we have?" (v. 47).

In Acts 16, Lydia was baptized after her conversion:

"One of those listening was a woman named Lydia, a dealer in purple cloth from the city of Thyatira, who was a worshiper of God. The Lord opened her heart to respond to Paul's message. When she and the members of her household were baptized, she invited us to her home. 'If you have judged me to be faithful to the Lord, come to my house and stay.' So she persuaded us" (v. 15).

In the same chapter the Philippian jailer was gloriously saved and immediately baptized:

"He then brought them out and asked, 'Sirs, what must I do to be saved?'"

"They replied, 'So they said, 'Believe on the Lord Jesus Christ, and you will be saved, you and your household.' Then they spoke the word of the Lord to him and to all who were in his house. And he took them the same hour of the night and washed their stripes. And immediately he and all his family were baptized" (Acts 16:30–33).

What is baptism? It is a picture of death to the old life and resurrection to walk in newness of life (see Rom. 6:4).

The truth of Scripture is you should be baptized as a confession of your faith as soon as possible after conversion. First there is *conviction* (Acts 2:37). Then there is *conversion.* Then there is *confession* (Acts 2:38). Baptism is confession for the believer. The reason many churches do not have preservation in their membership, even though they may have participation and proclamation, is because of a lack of emphasis on the first step of obedience, which is baptism.

Why do Southern Baptists emphasize baptism so much? It is not because the water will wash away a single sin, but it is vitally important to spiritual growth and preservation. If we are not obedient to the first step of Christian growth, how are we ever going to grow? If we do not live up to the light God gives us, how are we going to expect any more light? It is no wonder that more Christians do not grow in the grace and knowledge of our Lord. So many say, "Well, I'm going to think about baptism for a while." Baptism is an essential step in preservation and Christian growth. GuideStone #3 points us to the danger of de-emphasis upon baptism that is prevalent in many of the New Trendy gospel churches. In the New Testament church it was a high priority and important step in the preservation of new believers.

What is true New Testament baptism? It is best illustrated with the wedding ring. While wearing a wedding ring does not make one married, it certainly is an indication that one has made that commitment. On July 24, 1970, my wife gave me a wedding ring as we stood publicly at a wedding altar and committed our lives to each other. I have worn that ring every day since as a means of identification regarding that commitment. She could have given me my wedding ring three months before we were married, and I could have worn it, but it would have meant nothing. Many people have been baptized before they made their commitment to Christ. Believer's baptism must be subsequent to our time of commitment as a confession of such.

Baptism is commanded in the Great Commission (Matt. 28:19–20). It is the first public act of the believer in his confession of faith in Christ. It is ordinarily the door into the visible, local church. It is the initial ordinance (Acts 2:41; Acts 8:12; 1 Cor. 12:12–14; 1 Pet. 3:21). The act of baptism involves a personal obligation on the part of the believer to promote the cause of Christ represented by the work of the church. The true New Testament church is a soul-saving, baptizing, teaching, preaching, evangelistic institution, and the baptized believer is now a part of that great, missionary, worldwide ministry. We are united by the Spirit in the worship of God in praise, in thanksgiving, in prayer, and in the diffusion of the saving message of Christ to every creature. We are joined together in the body of our Lord for instruction, for spiritual growth, and for mutual help-fulness. It is a great, glorious, mighty, significant day when we are baptized into the body of Christ, the bride and church of our Lord.[1]

What then is the mode of New Testament baptism? The Greek word found here in the text is *baptizo*. It means to plunge, dip, submerge, or put under. It is used no fewer than 74 times in the New Testament. This particular word which means to put under is not only found in the New Testament, it is extensively used in Greek literature. In Greek literature the word *baptizo* meant, in some cases, to suffer shipwreck, to sink, or to perish in the water. The story is told of a Greek sea captain whose vessel was going down and he broadcast this "Mayday" message, "Baptizo, baptizo!" (I'm sinking. I'm sinking!) Since our Lord has commanded us to be baptized, it is certainly imperative that we should desire the proper New Testament mode. This mode of baptism is immersion.

The word in the original language, found in Acts 2:41, means to immerse. It is as plain as the nose on your face when you read the Scripture. We read that baptism required "much water." Take, for example, John 3:23 " Now John also was baptizing in Aenon near Salim, because there was much water there. And they came and were baptized." Baptism is described as a "going down into the water."

"And he ordered the chariot to stop. Then both Philip and the eunuch went down into the water and Philip baptized him" (Acts 8:38).

New Testament baptism is like a "burial" under the water.

"Therefore we were buried with Him through baptism into death, that just as Christ was raised from the dead by the glory of the Father, even so we also should walk in newness of life" (Rom. 6:4).

"Now if we died with Christ, we believe that we shall also live with Him" (Rom. 6:8).

New Testament baptism is described as coming up out of the water. " When He had been baptized, Jesus came up immediately from the water; and behold, the heavens were opened to Him, and He saw the Spirit of God descending like a dove and alighting upon Him" (Matt. 3:16).

*The crystal-clear truth of Scripture is that baptism is by immersion.* And it should always follow salvation! If you have not been immersed since your salvation experience you have not undergone New Testament baptism. This is not the view of any particular church. It is the truth of Scripture. Baptism should take place after salvation and not before. Note the order in Acts 2:38, "Repent and be baptized." The same order is found in Acts 2:41: " Then those who gladly received his word were baptized."

There are churches which practice infant baptism. Some churches baptize babies and very young children who have not yet had a genuine salvation experience. Many of these churches use Acts 2:39 as a proof text which goes: "For the promise is to you and to your children, and to all who are afar off, as many as the Lord our God will call." They claim infants should be baptized. But what does Acts 2:39 really teach? Read it carefully. Some take this verse and put a period after the word "children" so that it reads, "The promise is to you and to your children." Thus, they insist infants ought to be sprinkled; their argument being that the blessings of the covenant are for them and their children. But you cannot chop off a verse halfway and make it fit your own personal philosophy of theology.[2]

What is Acts 2:39 actually conveying? Look at it carefully. " For the promise is to you and to your children, *and* to all who are afar off, as many as the Lord our God will call." (author's italics). It is not only for you and your children, it is for those who are "far off." So then I may argue, "The promise is to you and to your children": therefore your children should be baptized. If we go on with the text, "and for all who are afar off," then all who are afar off should also be baptized. Therefore, we would be saying, all who are afar off should be baptized whether they are saved or not. So goes this reasoning, and it is completely unbiblical!

What does this text actually mean? It is pointing out that this covenant promise, " whosoever shall call on the name of the Lord shall be saved" (Acts 2:21, KJV), is meant for you and your children…and for those who are far off — the African natives, the negritos of New Guinea, the ebony-faced women of Ghana, the Eskimos in their igloos in Alaska, and anybody anywhere "to whom the Lord our God will call" is addressed. Someone quickly replies, "but whole households were baptized in the Book of Acts." Yes, but there is no scriptural reason to believe that in any case they did not first repent as Peter had preached in Acts 2:38. And after they had done this, then they were baptized!

Imagine the effect on Jerusalem when 3,000 people came out of the shadows to identify with the Lord Jesus Christ through believer's baptism. It is no wonder the whole city was stirred and moved. It is no wonder spiritual awakening came to Jerusalem. The first step in preserving new converts is to see them through the waters of baptism. Peter unapologetically and personally appealed to his hearers to be baptized. Every church should exhort their converts to be baptized, not because the water would save them or wash away their sins, but because it is the first step in preservation, growing in the grace and knowledge of our Lord. The truth is if we do not live up to the light God has given us, we can never expect to receive any more light.

Baptism is a means of identification. There is a prevalent trend in our culture. People today like to identify with certain things or persons. Some people wear keyrings with Mercedes Benz emblems, while others wear Gucci shoes with its emblem. Still others would not think of carrying anything but a Mont Blanc pen, while others wouldn't wear a tie that was not a Hermes. People like to identify with their schools so they wear a class ring or class sweater. There are some who would not wear a sweater that did not have the emblem of Ralph Lauren. There are still others who are quick to identify with certain watches.

Baptism gives us an opportunity to do what we like to do. That is, identify with something. Or, rather in this case, someone! Baptism is a means of identification. It lets the world know we have identified with Jesus Christ. What makes a church great in the eyes of God? *The power of the gospel, the proclamation of the gospel,* and *preservation of the gospel.* The first step in preservation is *baptism.*

## The Bible

The second step in preservation is the Bible. "And they continued steadfastly in the apostles' doctrine" (Acts 2:42). That is, they continued in the Word of God. The word *didache* means doctrine.

This consisted of the fundamentals of the faith. They

devoted themselves to such great doctrinal truths as the virgin birth of Christ, His sinless life and vicarious death, His bodily resurrection, and His second coming. They grounded themselves and continued in the great doctrinal truths of the Word of God.

We are not called merely to make decisions; we are called to make disciples. When a person is genuinely saved, one "continues in the apostles' doctrine." Our Lord Himself observed, "By their fruits you shall know them." There can be no preservation in the church where the Bible, and its doctrine and teaching, are not expounded and explained to the people. Many wonder why membership dwindles in some churches. It is because God blesses His Word, and when it is not used, there is no preservation. The church exploded in Jerusalem because they continued steadfastly "in the apostles' doctrine." They were rooted and grounded in the Word of God. Our only hope for preservation is the Word of God. You cannot grow in faith without that Word. You may be saved and be baptized, but if you do not devote yourself to the apostles' teaching, you will never grow in the grace and knowledge of Jesus Christ.

Paul wrote to Timothy that the Word of God was "profitable for doctrine, reproof, correction and instruction in righteousness." This is throughout the Scriptures. In Romans, the Bible is profitable for *doctrine*. In the

Corinthian letters, the Bible is profitable for *reproof.* In Galatians, the Bible is profitable for *correction.* In Ephesians, it is profitable for *instruction in righteousness.*

The Bible is like God's road map. *First, there is doctrine.* We begin down the road with Christ, and we face the amazing doctrinal truth of the Deity of Christ. He is God. When we obey and come to Christ, we are walking on the road with Him. But what happens when we veer along the road? *We see secondly that the Bible is profitable for reproof.* It reproves us and helps us recognize a wrong turn. God said, "Is not My word like a hammer that breaks the rock in pieces?" (Jer. 23:29). How does one straighten out one's path? *Here we find the Bible is profitable for correction.* The Word shows us how to get back on track with God, but it doesn't leave us there. *Finally, it is profitable for instruction in righteousness* (2 Tim. 3:16–17). The Word shows us how to stay on the road so we will not wander off again. It is profitable and essential in our preservation and growth.

On the night shift a young bivocational preacher was using his New Testament to witness during the company's 11:00 p.m. break. One of the listeners commented, "Yeah, just look at that guy leaning on his crutch."

To that the preacher replied, "You're right. It's my life-long crutch, and I can't do anything without leaning on it! It's life-giving, powerful, and sharper than a two-edged sword. Yes, it's my crutch. It's a crutch for poor, crippled sinners, and it'll boost them into heaven!"

"What if I say —

'The Bible is God's Holy Word,

Complete, inspired, without a flaw' —

But let its pages stay,

Unread from day to day,

And fail to learn there from God's law;

What if I go out there to seek

The truth of which I glibly speak,

For guidance on this earthly way, —

Does it matter what I say?"[3]

What makes a church great? The preservation of the gospel entails making much of baptism and much of the Bible.

## Body life

The third important element in preservation is body life. This body life concept is found in Acts 2:42–46:

"And they continued steadfastly in the apostles' doctrine and fellowship, in the breaking of bread, and in prayers. Then fear came upon every soul, and many wonders and signs were done through the apostles. Now all who believed were together, and had all things in common, and sold their possessions and goods, and divided them among all, as anyone had need.

So continuing daily with one accord in the temple, and breaking bread from house to house, they ate their food with gladness and simplicity of heart."

These people spent their time learning, loving, and listening to each other. Great churches are characterized by this body life concept. Every member is a minister and everyone functions within the body together. There was fellowship in this early church. "They continued steadfastly in the apostles' doctrine and *fellowship*" (Acts 2:42, author's italics). The word is *koinonia*. It means they were "all together" and they loved each other. It was one for all and all for one. It was a shared life.

The origin of the word *koinos* (from which *koinonia* is derived) means common, not in the sense we often think of today. It meant that which people share or have together. Consider the phrase, "and they had all things common" in relation to the Jerusalem church. Even in our current generation we often use the phrase, "We or they have such and such in common." It implies a like trait or characteristic.

All of us are familiar with metal money which is called a coin or coins. Those terms are straight from the Greek language. What is a coin used for? It is used for exchange, and it passes from hand to hand. Those who have phobias about germs probably think about a quarter, half dollar, or even pennies as possibly being soiled, because they have passed from hand to hand. A coin is a common piece shared by perhaps hundreds, maybe even thousands of hands.

Thus, it is with the *koinonia* we have in Christ. *Koinonia* ideally means, not merely fellowship, but a life which is shared. Every born-again believer has a common Savior, faith, experience, goal and destiny. Wherever you meet another genuine Christian, you have an immediate spiritual tie. If only we could remember this, churches would have virtually no real problems because all Christians are together through "the scarlet thread" of the blood of Jesus Christ which has drawn us and sewn us together into God's tapestry of the redeemed.

*Koinonia* is not merely coming together to have a meal or to participate in church activities. When a person is born again into God's family, he immediately has a kinship to every believer here and in the hereafter!

What happened? The coming and filling of the Holy Spirit caused them to live life on a higher plane of love for God and for one another. There are different Greek words which are translated into our English Bible with the word *love*. There is the word *agape* which means giving, forgiving, unreserved, or selfless — God's love. There is also *philos* which means tender affection, the brotherly sort of love. Prior to Pentecost, the best the apostles could do was to love on the level *of philos*. In fact, that is the best anyone can do without the Holy Spirit in his or her heart.

For example, you remember the conversation of our Lord Jesus with Simon Peter on the shore before Pentecost. John 21:15 records it. The Lord asked him, " Simon, son of Jonah, do you love Me more than these?" The word He used was *agape*.

Simon answered. "Yes, Lord, You know that I love You." Peter replied with the word *phileo*. It was the best Peter could do.[4]

Then on the night before the crucifixion, Jesus instructed His apostles,

"A new commandment I give to you, that you love one another; as I have loved you, that you also love one another. By this all will know that you are My disciples, if you have love for one another" (John 13:34–35).

Here is the word *agape*. Jesus was leaving His followers. They had watched His life for three years and up until then, the best they could do was to love on the level *of philos* love. It was the level of the old commandment which taught to "love your neighbor as yourself" " (Lev. 19:18). But now, love was not an option. It was to be a new commandment. It was to be *agape* and not philos. The point is this: Prior to Pentecost one could not love properly with God's love, because it is impossible without the Spirit's love burning within us. This love came into the disciples when they were filled with the Holy Spirit, and thus they "continued steadfastly in…fellowship." This is why Paul later wrote in Galatians 5:22, "the fruit of the Spirit is love" *(agape)*.

There was a legend that a rich merchant scoured the Mediterranean world looking for the distinguished apostle Paul. He encountered Timothy, the legend goes, who arranged a visit with Paul, who was a prisoner in Rome at that time.

Entering the jail cell, the merchant found a rather old man, physically broken down. The merchant was amazed at Paul's personal peace and serenity. The story goes that they talked for hours. The merchant left with Paul's blessing and prayer on his heart and mind. Outside the concerned merchant inquired, "What is the key to Paul's power? I have never seen anyone like him in my entire life."

"Haven't you figured it out?" asked Timothy. "Paul is in love."

The businessman with bewilderment asked, "In love?"

"Yes," Timothy answered, "Paul is in love with Jesus Christ."

The man looked even more confused. "Is that all?" he further inquired.

With a smile on his face, the young preacher answered,

"Ah, but that is everything."

This has so many applications. For example, this is why it is essential for a Christian to marry another believer and not an unbeliever. Try as he may, an unbeliever can never love a *mate* with the highest level of love, the most selfless kind of love *(agape),* because it is only found in Jesus Christ.

We need each other. Great churches are made up of great fellowship. We can be baptized and be in the Bible but still cannot grow without this concept of body life — *fellowship.* We need each other. There has never been a great church in the eyes of God without this element of fellowship. Some "professed believers" have such little fellowship with the people of God. We all ought to ask ourselves if we are merely singing hymns, saying words, and coming to meetings, just going through the motions. Some of us live like the world, think like the world, talk like the world, act like the world, and then go to church, watch our watches, and if the service goes over an hour we fidget. At the same time, we can go to a ball game, movie, or party and say, "How time flies," when we have been there three hours or more. And you tell me you are going to go to heaven, praise the Lord, and fellowship with the people of God there when you don't desire that fellowship here. Who are you kidding?

What makes a great church? Preservation involves baptism, the Bible, and body life. The first part of body life is *fel-*

*lowship,* but there is also the importance of the *"breaking of bread"* (Acts 2:42, author's italics). That is the Lord's Supper. Luke does not simply refer to having meals together. He makes the point that the early church came together to share in the symbolic testimony of the body and blood of Christ which is the basis of the Christian life. What is the breaking of bread? It is the Lord's Supper — the unleavened bread and the cup of unfermented juice from the vine. We have continued in this until this very day. It is a part of our preservation.

"Thy supper, Lord, before us spread,

The cup beside the broken bread,

Reminds us of Thy life laid down —

The shameful cross, the thorny crown.

Thy sacrifice was for our gain;

To save us Thou didst bear the pain.

Thy love is clear for all to see;

We bow in thankful prayer to Thee.

In fellowship with Thee we feel

That Thou art here, Thy presence real;

Thou hast risen and dost live

Within our hearts, new life to give

Now may the worship we know here

Remind us always thou art near;

Help us to live our lives each day

In love and faith, O Lord, we pray."

*Author Unknown*

*They also continued steadfastly in "prayer"* (see Acts 2:42).
They continued in prayer. This is how they began. For 10 days
they prayed in the upper room. Some of us begin but never
continue. Please note that they "continued steadfastly" in
prayer, not just in teaching, fellowship, and breaking of bread,
but in prayer, beseeching the Lord at the throne of grace.

These early believers "continued steadfastly in prayers."
Prayer is the cradle of revival. Jesus said, "My house shall
be called the house of prayer." So many believers get dressed
up in the whole armor of God of Ephesians 6. We put on
the helmet of salvation and the breastplate of righteousness
while holding the shield of faith and the sword of the Spirit
which is the Word of God. We also have around our loins
the girdle of truth and on our feet shoes with the prepara-
tion of the gospel of peace. We are ready to go for God.

But the problem often lies in the fact that many of us
don't even know where the battle is being fought. After
telling us all the pieces of the armor, Paul links armor with
prayer in the next verse "Praying always with all prayer and
supplication in the Spirit" (Eph. 6:18, KJV).

Prayer is the battlefield of the Christian life. It is impossible to win a war unless we march to the field. Consequently, the most important ministry of a local church
should be the ministry of prayer. The most important
room in all of the physical facilities of the church ought to

be the intercessory prayer chapel, where many people "stand in the gap" and intercede to the Father on behalf of members and ministries.

In fact, before every great undertaking, we should have days of prayer and fasting. The first committee appointed during a multimillion-dollar building program we had in our church was a prayer committee which continually kept prayer needs before our people week by week. Our Sunday morning services began with our men on their knees at the altar beseeching the God of heaven for His power to fall upon us. Our Wednesday evening services concluded with scores of people at the altar praying for the lost and for physical, emotional, and spiritual needs as we "pray for one another." *Yes,* Jesus said that His house was to be called "the house of prayer." The heart-cry, "Revive us again," will never be realized unless if is ushered in on the wings of personal intercessory prayer.

*They also had a sharing spirit.* Acts 2:42–44 says,

"And they continued steadfastly in the apostles' doctrine and fellowship, in the breaking of bread, and in prayers. Then fear came upon every soul, and many wonders and signs were done through the apostles. Now all who believed were together, and had all things in common."

They had the theme that every member was a minister. I doubt if they said, "Let Peter do it" or "Let's let Joseph of Arimathea pull a string with the United Way of Jerusalem." Everyone was together, and they all did their part.

Some contend that this sounds like communism. This was not communism in Acts 2. These people believed in God; this was church-controlled and not state-controlled; it was voluntary; and it was obviously temporary. Many Jews were away from home in Jerusalem for the Passover Feast. We do not read about it happening later in the early church, but the point is they had this concept of body life! What is the difference in what we see here and in communism today? Communism says, "What's yours is mine." This sharing in the Jerusalem church stated, "What's mine is yours."[5] And this is a stark difference! And that is why communism crumbled all over the world in our lifetime.

Everything the believers owned was at God's disposal when needed. This is the point. Is everything we own at God's disposal today? What if God were to impress upon your heart to give a certain amount of your stock portfolio or your real estate holdings? What if God were to impress upon you to give that precious possession to share it with the fellowship of believers?

Another concept of body life was "gladness and simplicity of heart," (Acts 2:46, KJV). This was a joyful church.

A gloomy Christian is a contradiction in terms. Joy filled the atmosphere of the presence of these people at Pentecost.

Another aspect of their body life was worship and praise (Acts 2:46–47). Praise is the secret of the liberated life! There is power in praise. "God inhabits the praises of his people," and we are to praise Him in song, word, and action. The truth is we cannot grow in grace and knowledge of our Lord without being involved in personal praise. In Ephesians 5:18, we find the command, "be filled with the Spirit," and in the next verse we notice the result in "singing and making melody in our hearts to the Lord" (Eph. 5:19, KJV).

These early believers lived in an atmosphere of the fear of God. The Bible records that at Pentecost "fear came upon all of them" (Acts 2:43). They lived their lives in an environment of the awareness of the reverential awe of a Holy God. Later the scripture records, "Then the church throughout all Jerusalem, Judea and Galilee had peace and was edified; and walking in the fear of the Lord and the comfort of the Holy Spirit, they were multiplied" (Acts 9:31). Multiplied! What did they learn that somehow we have forgotten? They were "walking in the fear of the Lord." For the Jerusalem church it was not the fear that God might put His hand of retribution on them but the fear that he might take His hand of anointing and blessing off of them! Who is talking about walking in the fear of the Lord today? We don't hear it in church growth conferences and yet, it is on virtually every page of the book of Acts. I believe it was one of the secrets to the explosive growth of the New Testament church of the first century.

In the midst of a church world where many advocates of the New Trendy gospel attend church services without so much as even carrying a Bible (perhaps because it is seldom used in worship experiences) it does us well to pause a moment along the road back to Jerusalem at this third guidestone and be reminded that the preservation of the gospel is about "continuing in the apostles' doctrine." We are "stewards" of these eternal truths and it remains to be seen what kind of "gospel" the second and third generations of much of modern church growth will have left. Among the dangers that GuideStone #3 identifies is the new "networks" of churches that are springing up with the New Trendy gospel movement. When you examine them closely, you find that the emphasis placed on their "networking" is not on what they believe, but is almost exclusively centered in methodology. This is ultimately one of the most dangerous elements of the New Trendy gospel. Throughout the centuries the church has marched triumphantly from generation to generation not because its fabric has been woven with threads of methodology but because of the scarlet thread of doctrinal truth which has been passed from generation to generation for centuries. Never before have such influential church leaders of the evangelical world built large followings that have placed methodology over doctrine. Our spiritual forefathers "continued". How? With, in, and through the doctrinal truths which have given us the New Testament gospel.

These early church leaders foresaw this danger and subsequently in the second chapter of Acts set up GuideStone #3 to forever remind us of the importance of doctrinal truth in preserving the gospel of our Lord Jesus Christ.

GuideStone #4

# The propagation of the gospel

*(Acts 2:47)*

A long the road of our journey back to Jerusalem we, at last, come to GuideStone #4. This ancient marker, like the others, has been left for us by our spiritual forefathers in order to point direction and warn of dangers. This marker admonishes us about the importance of personally sharing the gospel with those with whom we come in contact. Some refer to this today as "confrontational evangelism." I am the product of this approach. I am forever grateful that after a basketball game during my senior year in high school, a young man approached me in the parking lot and boldly and winsomely confronted me with the good news of the Lord Jesus Christ. Tragically, the call of much of modern church growth today has a de-emphasis on this type of evangelism as is evidenced by a void of training in this regard.

Perhaps there is no other place where the Jerusalem church of the first century is more diametrically different from the western church of the 21st century than in this issue of confrontational evangelism. Throughout every page of the Book of Acts we find these early believers boldly engaging and confronting individuals from all walks of life with the gospel. In fact, in so doing, the Bible goes so far as to say they "turned their world upside down."

Contrast this New Testament approach to the New Trendy approach of a recent church start in the Dallas-Fort Worth metroplex where I live. This church circulated a direct mass mailing promotion to thousands of homes in their area. Across the top of the mailing it says, "Top Ten Reasons to Avoid Church." Note some of these "top ten" promises this church is making to people in this clever little mailing.

One promise is this — "If you come to our church it will all be over in an hour and you will still have plenty of time to enjoy the day." That is their offer. Can you imagine the Lord Jesus saying to those multitudes in Galilee, "Just give me a few minutes and then you can get it over with and go enjoy the rest of the day?"

The mailing also promises to "not make you listen to

a bunch of old songs and an organ." I found that a bit strange since the scripture says we are to praise him on "stringed instruments and organs." The early church had Psalms which they sang in worship. That was pretty old stuff even in the first century.

How about this promise made by this New Trendy gospel church — "You can leave your wallet at home. We promise not to talk to you about money." Now, that is a real motivation for discipleship isn't it? Isn't there something in the Bible about "honoring the Lord with the first fruits of our increase"? Can you imagine the Lord Jesus saying, "Follow me and keep your money and everything else to yourself"? He said, "Where your treasure is there your heart will be also!"

The promises continued, "You can blend in with our people and not be recognized." Can you imagine Simon Peter making such an appeal to the people in Jerusalem? Can you imagine our Lord who said, "Come out from among them and be separate" saying, "if you will come to my church you can blend right in with everyone else, redeemed or lost, it doesn't matter"?

Here is a real motivation — "We will give you coffee and donuts free."

But, one of the strangest of all promises was the one which said, "We promise not to visit you." Strange, since our model church in Jerusalem was going everywhere in the market place sharing the good news of Christ. The Lord Jesus, who admonished us to go out into the highways and hedges and compel men and women to come to faith, would never make such an absurd promise in the name of His church.

There are many churches of all stripes today who do little or nothing to proclaim the substitutionary atonement and the death of Christ to a lost world. It is seldom even mentioned. Would to God we could hear Pastor Peter's commentary on this seeker friendly approach. He was beaten. He was threatened to never speak again in the name of Christ. What did he do? He went away rejoicing that he was counted worthy to suffer in His name. He left us a guidestone along the way to remind us of the importance of the propagation of the gospel.

And what about Paul? Thank God he did not buy into this New Trendy approach. He was stoned at Lystra and left for dead. He was ship wrecked at Malta. He was beaten in Philippi. He was thrown in jail in numerous places and finally martyred in Rome. Can you see him trying to build the church at Philippi or at Ephesus or wherever he went by promising to give away "free coffee and donuts"? Can you imagine this great church planter offering a type of gospel that simply entertained and met "felt needs" without compelling anyone to bear a cross? No, never. His was a New Testament gospel.

One of the heroes of the modern church growth movement of the last few decades said the following in an interview published in *Christianity Today* magazine on October 5, 1984, "I don't think anything has been done in the name of Christ and under the banner of Christianity that has proven more destructive to human personality and hence counterproductive to the evangelistic enterprise than the unchristian, uncouth strategy of attempting to make people aware of their lost and sinful condition." In other words, don't do anything to offend the seeker. What a contrast we see in Acts 2 when Peter confronts men and women with their sin and "their hearts are cut".

These are not isolated illustrations in modern church growth. Such ideology is rampant when we open our eyes. For example, I came across an interesting book which I purchased from a Baptist divinity school bookstore on the campus of a Baptist university (formerly Southern Baptist I might add). It was written by someone who was formerly a professor of a Baptist university in the south. The book has a fascinating title — *Ten Things I Learned Wrong from a Conservative Church*. Chapter three is titled — "Third Wrong Teaching: Jesus is the Only Way to God." The following is a direct quote from the chapter, "Baptists and other dyed-in-the-wool conservatives have this thing about Jesus, that since the incarnation 2,000 years ago he is the only way to God." He does not put much stock in John's gospel either. In fact, he insinuates that the "Jesus" of the fourth gospel was "arrogant" by stating he was the way, the truth and the life. But there is more, he goes on to say, "I don't think it is necessary for people to have an experience with Christ in order to enter the Kingdom of Heaven."

We are living in a day when the gospel is under attack. And not just from without, but in some places from within. This issue of the exclusivity of Christ and the gospel message is the burning issue of our day. Let's pause a moment at this fourth guidestone and see the importance of recovering a passion for the propagation of the gospel in our lifetime. These early believers were "praising God and having favor with all the people. And the Lord added to the church daily those who were being saved" (Acts 2:47).

A church can have power, proclamation, and preservation, but if the church does not have the element of propagation, it will never be a great church in the eyes of God. This early church went everywhere witnessing. The propagation of the gospel fulfilled Acts 1:8 in one day. And the result was the "Lord added to their number daily those who were being saved." They propagated the gospel in a winsome way and a winning way.

If we are ever to see the church truly revived again in our generation, then we must lay hold of this concept of equipping the saints to do the work of the ministry. This first-century church went everywhere sharing their faith and performing the works of ministry.

The churches in our day and age who are seeing mercy drops of revival are those who have mobilized their people to do the work of ministry. These are churches which have all kinds of ministries but only one overriding purpose, and that is to glorify and honor the Lord Jesus by fulfilling the Great Commission to make, mark, and mature believers in the faith.

## Example

To begin with, mobilization is done by example. If pastors are going to mobilize their people as we move the church, then we must be on the cutting edge ourselves, and our people must see that we do not ask them to do something we are too good to do ourselves. The best way to mobilize people for the work of ministry is by *example*. Perhaps Gideon expressed it best when, as he led his small army to face the Midianites, he said, "Do as I do!" These pointed words may be the epitaph of many churches today. That is, they do what the pastor does. My pastor, Fred Swank, used to tell all of his preacher boys: "Never use your people to build your ministry, but always use your ministry to build your people."

## Expectancy

Another important element in the mobilization of people to the work of the ministry is expectancy. Here is the spirit of conquest. A vision, if you please. Someone has commented that a "vision without a task is simply a dream. A task without a vision is drudgery. But a vision with a task is the hope of the world."

The birth of a vision is like the birth of a baby. It begins with conception. The seed of a vision is conceived in the leader's heart by the Lord Himself. The next step is gestation. Here the vision grows inside us. After a while those around us can see that something is growing within us. This is the stage where we meditate, pray, yes; gestate the vision that has been conceived in us. Then comes the stage of birth. This is when we share our vision with others. It is out in the open. The next step is one of the most vital. It is the step of adoption when those others who have not personally birthed much less gestated and conceived the vision adopt it as though it was their very own. Then comes the stage of growth. Just like when our children are growing they cause challenges and cost money. So it is when the vision that has been adopted by others continues to grow. Next comes the step of maturity when all we have prayed for and dreamed about comes to fruition. Finally, there is the stage of reproduction. At this stage many who have seen their vision come to maturity never dream again. This is a critical stage that begins the process all over again. All of this has to do with creating the element of expectancy in the lives of our people in the churches. People want to be a part of something that is going somewhere with a direction and a dynamic.

## Environment

Another key element in the mobilization of people to propagate the gospel is found in the word *environment*. In my opinion the two greatest factors in church growth are love and unity among the fellowship. This hurting, wounded world is looking for true love and true unity.

On the evening before the crucifixion, Jesus said, "A new commandment I give unto you. That ye love one another; as *I have loved you*" (John 13:34, KJV, author's italics). For 33 years Jesus had given us a picture of what real love truly is. Up until then, the best we could do was live on the level of the old commandment found in Leviticus 19:18, "Love your neighbor as yourself." But some of us have a real problem there. That is, we have no self-worth or self-respect, and if we loved others as we love ourselves, we wouldn't be loving with very deep love. But after 33 years of demonstrating what true love really is, Jesus said, "Love one another as I have loved you." The environment of love is the most important ingredient in church growth, and it is also the most basic factor in mobilizing people to propagate the gospel.

Not only is love important to the environment but also to unity. I believe the pastor's primary job is to "maintain the unity of the spirit and the bond of peace." Personally, this is what I guarded more than all else during my pastoral days. The most important factor in a family is unity. The most important factor in an athletic team is unity. The most important factor in a business is unity. And a church should be known by its unity. I am not speaking about uniformity but unity. There is a tremendous difference. Uniformity is an outward expression while unity is an inward expression. Cults emphasize uniformity, not unity. There is diversity in unity. We are not all alike, but we can all be together.

## Exertion

Another important word in mobilizing people to the propagation of the gospel is exertion. We are to equip the saints to do "the work of the ministry." And the ministry is work! When we are truly walking in the Spirit, we will not be wearing out the seats of our pants but the soles of our shoes. So often I hear that this church or that church simply operates "in the flesh." Well, the fact is, that is what our Spirit-filled lives have to operate within.

Do you know how hot and humid it can be in Fort Lauderdale in August? Our staff would go on evangelism visits every Saturday. Often when I would pull up in front of someone's house to share Jesus Christ only to have a door slammed in my face or to have someone rudely cut me off, my flesh would not advise me to keep doing that. My flesh would tell me to go back home and sit under the air conditioner or lie down on a mat in the swimming pool. My flesh never told me to do anything for Christ. People will respond to exertion. They want to be a part of something exciting.

As we follow the life of Jesus, we discover that He exerted Himself so many times in so many ways. He had a special affinity toward the outcast. Jesus loves the rejects and pariahs of society. When He went to Jerusalem, where did He go? To the pool of Bethesda where handicapped persons were lying near the pool. When He went through Jericho where did He go? Did He make a beeline to meet the mayor to receive the key to the city? No, He went to a blind beggar rattling a cup on the side of the road. When He passed through Samaria did He have an "I-know-the-governor syndrome" like so many of us preachers today? No, He didn't go to the governor. He was interested in a sinful woman outside the city at Jacob's Well. He met her in the middle of the day to give her living water. Some of us need to stop being so hypocritical as we sit pompously behind our stained-glass walls talking about how much we care about missions in Africa when we are uncomfortable having a Haitian refugee sitting beside us on the pew. Revival comes when folks do not mind getting their hands dirty in something that is real.

## Encouragement

We also find that another element of mobilizing people to the propagation of the gospel is encouragement. Nothing mobilizes people more than encouragement, words of appreciation, exhortation, and encouragement. As we read the Book of Acts, we find those early believers continually encouraging one another in the faith. If the church is going to be revived again in our day, it is not enough simply to have the element of power or proclamation or preservation. We must become caught up in propagation and burst outside the four walls of our buildings, mobilizing our people to do the work of the ministry and carrying the gospel to the four corners of the world!

*Note that they propagated the gospel in a winsome way.* The Bible says they were " having favor with all the people" (Acts 2:47). The religious system of the day rejected these early believers. They were a threat to the traditional religion. Also, the Roman government rejected them because they would not bow down and say, "Caesar is Lord." But the truth is that most of the people embraced them. They "had favor with all the people." They were winsome in their witness and in their worship, and thousands were converted because of it.

Real Christianity is lovely. There is a quality about a Spirit-filled, radiant Christian that draws and attracts others and causes them to "have favor with all the people." The truth is that the gospel is not nearly as offensive as some of its proponents! People were attracted to these early believers' joy and wanted to know the source of it. Evangelism in this first century church was more caught than taught. And, that is how it should be in the 21st century church.

*They also propagated the gospel in a winning way.* "And the Lord added to the church daily those who were being saved" (Acts 2:47). They were a growing church! Every once in awhile we hear someone remark, "I like to be part of a small, spiritual church." There is no such thing as a small, spiritual church in a metropolitan area. I understand that population makes a difference. If the church is spiritual, it will be healthy, and if it is healthy, it will be growing! If you are the type of person who does not want to be part of a large church, you certainly would not have wanted to be a member of the first church in Jerusalem in the first century.

What do I mean? Let's see! In Acts 1:15, there were 120 believers. Someone says, "Oh, we like it like that." There are many churches like that. They are sometimes governed by people who want something they can control. Often they cannot control anything at work or at home, so they might join a little church and develop a "God complex." They want to be served; they don't want to serve. They want a preacher to stroke them and pat them on the back. All the while the whole world is going to hell, and they want a church they can control. This early church was a healthy church, and because it was healthy it was filled with power, proclamation, preservation, and it propagated the gospel so it grew in grace and numbers into the multiplied thousands.

Here we see these early believers being faithful to our Lord's last words to them, "But you shall receive power when the Holy Spirit has come upon you; and you shall be witnesses to Me in Jerusalem, and in all Judea and Samaria, and to the end of the earth" (Acts 1:8).

They had come to grips with five important questions which had arisen out of these last words of our Lord. Now, having been endued with power from on high, they were fulfilling Acts 1:8 in their generation.

First, they dealt with the question of *who*. You! Here is an imperative in the future tense. No one was excluded. The point is, none of us are beyond this commission of Christ to be witnesses of His saving grace.

Next we deal with the question of *what*. They were to receive what? Power! Here is the urgent need of the church today. Many churches are anemic in their worship and in their witness. The word translated *power (dunamis)* is the same word from which we receive our word *dynamite*. As we have seen earlier, the difference in the first century church and the 21st century church is in two words — influence and power. While the church of our day prides itself in influence (particularly in the political realm), it has so little power. The early church did not have enough influence to keep Peter out of prison but had enough power to pray him out!

Next, they dealt with the question of *when*. When? When would this power come upon them? "When the Holy Spirit comes upon you." The Holy Spirit within is Who gives power. We need to strengthen our witness that comes from a source that is outside of us. We need the dynamic power of the Holy Spirit within us, and when we are being filled with the Holy Spirit, witnessing will become as natural as water running downhill. Like Peter and the other apostles, we cannot "help but speak the things we have seen and heard."

They also dealt with the question of *why*. Why were they to receive power when the Holy Spirit came upon them? There is only one reason — "To be my witnesses." If you are saved, you have Christ, and He has you. If you have Christ, you have the Holy Spirit. If you have the Holy Spirit, you have power. If you have power, you are a witness. Note that He does not fill us with the Holy Spirit in order for us to become the judge, prosecuting attorney, defense, or jury — but the witness.

We are witnesses unto Christ. We are not recruiters trying to induce people to join our club. We are not salesmen trying to sell people our products. We are not marketers trying to brand our product. We are witnesses of Jesus Christ and His saving grace. The mark of a carnal church is that it talks about itself and invites people to come hear its preacher or to attend its Sunday School. The mark of a mature church is that it talks about the Lord Jesus Christ and is a witness unto Him.

This early church also dealt with the question of *where.* Where is this gospel to be taken as we are filled with God's Holy Spirit? The gospel is to be taken across the city, across the country, across the continent, and across the cosmos. There is a sense in which Acts 1:8 is an outline for the rest of the book of Acts. They took the gospel to Jerusalem in Acts 1–8. They took the gospel through Judea and Samaria in Acts 9–12. They took the gospel to the ends of the earth in Acts 13–28. In 30 years this exciting early church fulfilled

Acts 1:8. There is an important point for the church of our day. We cannot play leapfrog with the Great Commission. Witnessing for Christ begins in our own Jerusalem, not the ends of the earth. The highest form of hypocrisy is for mission groups to talk about how much they want to win people to Christ on foreign fields when they will not even share Jesus Christ with their next-door neighbor. Propagating the gospel begins at home and continues until it reaches the end of the world!

Many lament that taking the gospel to the whole world is a mammoth task for the 21st century church. What a task it must have been for the first century church.

It looked *geographically* impossible. Many believed the world was still flat! It appeared to be *physically* impossible. There was no air travel, no printing press, no radio, no television, no telephone, no facsimile machine and no Internet. It looked *legally* impossible. It was against the law to speak in Christ's name in many places. It looked *socially* impossible. The church was made up of so many rejects and outcasts of society.

But how did they do it? Did they do it through a well devised marketing strategy? Did they do it by propagating positive thinking? They received power when the Holy Spirit came upon them and then they propagated the gospel to the ends of the world. They went empowered by

God's Spirit in them and it took them to where people were in need of the gospel of Jesus Christ.

The church must do this if it is ever going to be revived again. We need to remember Jesus did not die in a starched white shirt and an expensive tie on a gold cross on some mahogany communion table within the stained-glass walls of some high-steepled church. He died out there where thieves were cursing and soldiers were gambling, and that is where we are to go, "to the ends of the earth." We are to penetrate the whole world until "the darkness shall turn to dawning. And the dawning to noon day bright. And Christ's great kingdom shall come on earth, the kingdom of love and light."

By Acts 2:41, we read "three thousand were added to their number that day." Now there were 3,120. In Acts 2:47, it says, "And the Lord added to the church daily those who were being saved." In Acts 4:4, " the number of men grew to be about five thousand." The word for men used in Acts 4:4 is *andros.* It is a word used for man in the masculine sense as opposed to a woman. These were five thousand *men,* and it is likely their families were also saved. Some believe as many as 15 to 20,000 were saved by the time of this account in Acts 4:4. It is very possible then that the church numbered around 25,000 members. In Acts 5:28, we read that the message of Christ had "filled Jerusalem." Oh, what a day!

If only in America today, we might one day hear that our cities were filled with the good news of Jesus. In Acts 6:7, the King James translators rendered this verse to read "multiplied greatly." Now, we are no longer talking about addition but multiplication. How many were in the early church? While no one knows for sure, Dr. B. H. Carroll, the founder of Southwestern Baptist Theological Seminary, thought there were 65,000 members the first six months. G. Campbell Morgan, the late, great pastor of Westminster Chapel in London, figures there were 250,000 converted in the first six months of the church in Jerusalem. The point is they propagated the gospel in a winsome way and in a winning way.

What makes a church great in the eyes of God? Power, proclamation, preservation, and propagation. And we must have all four! There are some churches who have power. They live together in unity and make much of the filling of the Holy Spirit but have no preservation. There are others who have proclamation and make much of the Bible but who have no power, no sense of belonging to God, much less to one another. There are still others who make much of propagation but who have no sense of preservation of new converts. Great churches in the eyes of God, like the Jerusalem church, are characterized by a balanced ministry that involves all four elements. This is what the church needs today. Oh, that the church of Jesus Christ today would live together in unity, be filled with the Holy Spirit, make much of the Word of God in proclamation, preserve their new converts to grow in grace and knowledge through "the apostles' doctrine", and go outside the four walls of their church to propagate the gospel in a winsome and winning way. If this would only happen, our land would be filled with the message of Jesus Christ.

One of the blessings of my own personal devotional life is to pray the great hymns of the faith. As I concluded these writings of the early church I found myself praying through my spirit the words of that great old hymn:

"Lord, as of old at Pentecost
Thou didst Thy power display
With cleansing purifying flame
Descend on us today.
For mighty words for Thee
Prepare and strengthen every heart
Come, take possessions of Thine own
And never more depart.
All self consume, all sin destroy
With earnest zeal endue
Each waiting heart to work for Thee
O Lord, our faith renew.
Speak, Lord! Before Thy throne we wait
Thy promise we believe

And will not let thee go until
Thy blessing we receive.
Lord, send the old time power
The Pentecostal power
Thy flood gates of blessing
On us throw open wide.
Lord, send the old time power
The Pentecostal power
That sinners be converted
And Thy name glorified."

*Lyrics by Charles H. Gabriel*

May God's special blessings rest upon that church which manifests its ministry in power, proclamation, preservation, and propagation. And may our continual prayer be with that of the Psalmist: "O, that You would… revive us again!"

# POSTSCRIPT

A few years ago my wife, Susie, and I were spending a few days in Jerusalem. Early one morning we went to a place opposite the little road adjacent to the Garden of Gethsemane on the Mount of Olives to pray together. As we were sitting on a large rock I looked down and saw on a blade of grass what appeared to be little diamonds. Instinctively, I reached down and plucked it up. When I held it close to my eyes I could tell they were not diamonds at all, but drops of dew glistening in the early morning hours. To the surface of my mind came a verse of scripture I had memorized 30 years earlier and not given thought of in all those decades. It was Hosea 14:5 which is a promise from God saying, "I will be like the dew to Israel." As I looked at that blade of grass, the promise of God to "be like the dew" to His people captured me. Where does dew come from? Does it fall? Or, does it rise? Think about it. The answer is neither. It just appears when certain conditions are right. We have a word for it — condensation. What a promise from God! Does God fall on us? Or, rise to meet us. No. He just appears when certain conditions are right! Yes, He will be like "the dew" to His people.

There is so much that is good, needed and refreshing in modern church growth. This small volume has simply been an appeal that in the midst of our entire quest to be relevant to a culture around us that we not sacrifice our "ancient landmarks" in the process. While there is so much good in modern church growth, some of it carries with it some dangerous warning signs. I am speaking of a virtual void of the importance of the Holy Spirit's work in and through the church, a glaring de-emphasis of expository preaching, a blatant disregard for doctrinal truth, and discouragement away from confrontational evangelism.

Yes, when conditions are right, the Lord shows up! Knowing this, our spiritual forefathers in Jerusalem left us four guidestones as reminders to keep us pointed in the right direction and to warn us of dangers ahead. This is a call to remember the importance of the power of the gospel, the proclamation of the gospel, the preservation of the gospel and the propagation of the gospel.

All roads do, indeed, lead to Jerusalem. And, along the way, when conditions are right, God has promised to show up! Let the church be the church, let the people rejoice!

# NOTES

*Chapter I*
1. *Life Application Bible* (Wheaton, Ill.: Tyndale Publishers, Inc., 1986), 305.
2. Fritz Reinecker and Cleon Rogers, *Linguistic Key to the Greek New Testament* (Grand Rapids, Mich.: Zondervan Publishing House, 1976), 265.
3. W.A. Criswell, *Acts an Exposition* (Grand Rapids, Mich.: Zondervan Publishing House, 1978), 77–78.
4. Ibid., 79.

*Chapter 2*
1. Lloyd John Ogilvie, *Acts: The Communicator's Commentary* (Waco, TX: Word Books, 1983), 70.
2. Words, Gloria and William J. Gaither. © Copyright 1971 by William J. Gaither. All rights reserved. Used by permission.
3. C.H. Spurgeon, *The Treasure of the New Testament II* (Grand Rapids, Mich.: Zondervan Publishing House, 1950), 745.
4. O.S. Hawkins, *Where Angels Fear to Tread* (Nashville: Broadman Press, 1983), 84–85.
5. Reinecker and Rogers, 267.
6. L.R. Scarborough, *With Christ After the Lost* (Nashville: Broadman Press, 1955), 55–56.
7. Ibid., 64.
8. Ibid., 65–66.
9. Ogilvie, 72.
10. H.L. Wilmington, *Wilmington's Guide to the Bible* (Wheaton, Ill.: Tyndale House Publishers, Inc., 1981), 371.

11. Criswell, 96.

12. John F. Walvoord and Roy B. Zuck, *The Bible Knowledge Commentary* (Wheaton, III.: Victor Books, 1983), 359.

13. Fanny J. Crosby, "Rescue the Perishing" *Baptist Hymnal* (Nashville: Convention Press, 1975), 285.

14. W.A. Criswell, *Criswell's Guidebook for Pastors* (Nashville: Broadman Press, 1980), 237–38.

*Chapter 3*

1. Criswell, *Guidebook,* 203.

2. Spurgeon, 747.

3. Maud Frazer Jackson, *Masterpieces from Religious Verse,* ed. James Dalton Morrison (Nashville: Broadman Press, 1971), 383.

4. Ogilvie, 61.

5. Wilmington, 371.

# Become a life-long partner with GuideStone Financial Resources

If you serve in a church these paragraphs are unapologetically for you and they could be some of the most important paragraphs you will read. Although you will never "retire" from ministry, there will come a day when you will retire from vocational church service.

It is important to get started early in retirement planning. There is a thing called compound interest, which is extremely powerful. For example, assuming an 8% annual return, if a 25-year-old minister put $50 per month in his retirement account it would be worth $174,550 at age 65. If the same person waited until just the age of 35 to begin saving for retirement with the same $50 per month it would be worth $74,520 at age 65, a difference of $100,000. It is very important to start early, but it is also important to start wherever you are along the way to retirement.

Participants in eligible Southern Baptist churches receive an added benefit, the Protection Section, by being in GuideStone's church retirement program. If you or your Southern Baptist church contributes only a few dollars per month to your retirement, you automatically receive at no cost to you or your church, a survivor's benefit worth up to $100,000 to whomever you designate as your beneficiary. You also receive at no cost a $500 per month disability benefit simply by being a part of the church retirement program. This benefit is a cooperative effort provided by your state Baptist convention and GuideStone and is a safety net every Southern Baptist church should utilize for their ministers.

We at GuideStone want to be a life-long partner with you throughout your entire ministry. This is the driving reason behind products which give you additional opportunities to save for retirement, or whatever your saving needs might be. You have available to you savings vehicles in addition to your regular 403(b) plan that includes Personal Investing Accounts and IRAs (Traditional and Roth IRAs). These opportunities are also available to spouses of persons eligible to participate in GuideStone plans. Perhaps you have a retirement accumulation in a 401(k) plan from a previous employer. You may want to consider "rolling over" that accumulation into your retirement account or into a rollover IRA.

For more information about these personal investing products, housing allowance advantages in retirement, or any of our other services, visit us on the World Wide Web at *www.GuideStone.org* or better yet call us at **1-800-262-0511** and speak personally to one of our Customer Relations specialists.